THE EROSION OF EDUCATION
Socialization and the Schools

THE EROSION OF EDUCATION
Socialization and the Schools

David Nyberg
State University of New York at Buffalo

and

Kieran Egan
Simon Fraser University, British Columbia

Teachers College
Columbia University
New York and London, 1981

Published by Teachers College Press, 1234 Amsterdam Avenue, New York, N.Y. 10027

Library of Congress Cataloging in Publication Data

Nyberg, David, 1943-
    The erosion of education.

    Includes bibliographical references and index.
    1. Educational sociology.   2. Socialization.
I. Egan, Kieran.   II. Title.
LC191.N92   370.19   81-8983
                                AACR2
ISBN 0-8077-2666-4
ISBN 0-8077-2665-6 (paper)

Manufactured in the United States of America

86   85   84   83   82   81   1   2   3   4   5   6

The following material is reprinted by permission:

Parts of chapter one are from David Nyberg, "Basic Competence Testing: An Educational Sham," The English Record, XXIX, no. 4 (1978), 16–19, and Kieran Egan, "John Dewey and the Social Studies Curriculum," Theory and Research in Social Education, 8, no. 2 (1980).

Part of chapter two is from David Nyberg, "Education as Community Expression," Teachers College Record, 79. no. 2 (1977), 205–23.

Part of chapter four is from David Nyberg, "Skill School v. Education School: An Essay on Carl Bereiter's Pedagogics," Educational Theory, 26, no. 2 (1976), 214–22.

Parts of chapter five are from Educational Development by Kieran Egan. Copyright © 1979 by Oxford University Press, Inc. (used by permission) and adapted from Kieran Egan, "Towards an Educational Theory of Development," Educational Philosophy and Theory, 11, no. 2 (November 1979), University of New South Wales

Part of chapter nine is from David Nyberg, "On an Heroic Contribution to Useless Debate," Educational Theory, 23, no. 3 (1973), 260–66.

Excerpts in chapters two and four from Israel Scheffler, "Philosophical Models of Teaching," Harvard Educational Review, 34 (1965), 131–43. Copyright © 1965 by President and Fellows of Harvard College.

The authors would like to thank Eileen Mallory for doing a careful, efficient, and cheerful job when typing the manuscript.

For our children

Jon and Noah
Michael, Catherine, and David

Contents

Introduction

The theme of *crisis* seems central to modern consciousness. Problems within and between our cultures are perceived with urgency, attempts at diagnosis and remedy are desired and often made in great haste, and it seems that everything is going wrong at the same time, leaving us little chance to sort out what is best to do in the long run.

The observation that our public schools and other educational institutions are themselves "in crisis" is often made and loudly lamented. This observation may be met, however, with the further observation that this has been the case since the very beginnings of public education. "The crisis," it would seem, is perpetual. Still, it is possible to distinguish attributes of the present state of crisis from previous ones because there have been important changes in the actual roles that schools do (and are expected to) perform.

The change of roles that we have in mind, and which is the focus of this book, concerns a commonly recognized but seldom articulated distinction between the two things that schools do — socialize and educate. In broad terms, *socialization* refers to preparation for a life of gainful employment and participation in everyday social, economic, and political activities — active citizenship; *education* refers to a somewhat different and less practical set of dispositions and capacities to appreciate and enjoy those aspects of one's culture that include a historical perspective and the life of the mind.

We believe that schools ought to provide opportunities for both socialization and education, but we also believe that schools ought to distinguish more explicitly between these functions and take more care to protect against the erosion of education. We argue that schools are becoming places where the young are socialized but no longer educated, and that the traditional assumption that schools are also responsible for education is being eroded. This erosion of the educational role of schools is largely unrecognized because we casually call whatever goes on in schools "education." Our purpose in this book is to point out as clearly as we can a distinction between the legitimate socializing role of schools and their education role. Then by considering a range of issues affecting schools today, we show that there is an increasing dominance of the socializing role and a corresponding erosion of education. We also show that this shift is significant, has important implications for the future of our society, is undesirable, and should be redressed.

THE EROSION OF EDUCATION
Socialization and the Schools

CHAPTER ONE

Education and Socialization

WE WANT TO POINT OUT a confusion in North American educational studies that gets in the way of an effort to distinguish between education and socialization. It is a confusion also reflected in the design of curricula and in teaching practice. The confusion arises from the fact that education is a social process—it usually involves a teacher and students whose actions are related to each other in a common context where some form of cooperation is required—and from the fact that the schools, which are central educational institutions, serve social purposes. The problem comes about when the inference is drawn from these obvious facts that education is necessarily, and ought to be, a socializing process. John Dewey, most influentially, did not tire of emphasizing the desirability of making such an inference between social experience and the aims of education.

Schools socialize by necessity and are in that regard useful in helping people to make a living and in helping to serve the national interests of manpower, productivity, and stability. Schools have also traditionally sought to educate and are in that regard desirable, for the purpose of education is ultimately to develop a sense of the pleasures of appreciating and taking part in one's culture. A teacher can be trained to socialize (we have a social scientific technology for such instruction), but a teacher must be educated in order to educate. There will never be a technology of education in this sense of the term, because the ends and the means of education are essentially contestable—like freedom and justice and love. These most fundamental ideas yield to variable descriptions and various interpretations, and they cannot be contained by the requirements of any technology whose purpose is the efficient production of specified ends.

Our purpose in this opening chapter, then, is to etch as clearly as we can a useful distinction between educating and socializing, and to begin to look at some of the reasons why it is useful. In the rest of the book we use this distinction to reflect on a range of current practices in education, and to show that keeping the distinct roles of schools separate may help to resolve a number of practical problems.

A NEGLECTED DISTINCTION

Everyone, of course, makes some distinction between the educating and socializing functions of schools. These are functions that obviously overlap, but it is generally recognized that it is useful to hold some distinction between them. By socializing we mean those activities directed toward enabling students to perform as competent agents within their society; by educating we mean something in addition to this — that "something" is usually rather vague and difficult to specify in any detail, but it refers to a range of cultural attainments that do not serve any particular social end while enriching in some way the life of the person who acquires them. Being socialized, we may say, makes life in society possible; being educated makes it more worthwhile. We want schools to help achieve both socializing and educational aims, understanding that the former are necessary while the latter are merely desirable.

Socialization and education require different criteria in justifying curriculum activities. Socializing is regulated by the criterion of direct relevance or utility to social praxis. So, given the nature of our society, teaching children to read and write is justified on grounds of social utility, and learning such skills is an important component in the socializing process. Learning to read with refined critical discrimination and to write with style cannot be justified on criteria of direct social utility or relevance, but these skills may be justified on grounds of educational value. Similarly, learning some local, regional, and national history can be justified on socializing grounds— it is important for people to have a simple understanding of how their society functions and how it got that way. Developing a sophisticated historical consciousness cannot be justified on grounds of social utility, but may be justified on grounds of educational value.

We do not intend that socialization and education be treated as entirely distinct categories. Our aim here is not to stipulate new meanings for these terms, but simply to secure agreement that it is useful to maintain a clear distinction between socializing and educating activities. Clearly the two flow into each other at many points. Educational activities seem in many cases to emerge from socializing activities. Given the way we are making the distinction, one might say that education is impossible without socialization. But then we should add that they should not be seen simply as sequential activities —the first one socializing and then the other educating. It would be more reasonable to say that almost all activities in schools have socializing and educational dimensions. In woodworking or metalworking, for example, one can justify children's learning the use of tools and the abilities to make and fix things on clear socializing criteria. But these activities properly should also have an educational dimension, which will usually be connected with some aesthetic aspect of the work—the desire to do something well or beautifully or to have some quality above and beyond what pure practical utility calls for. Similarly in teaching writing, one rarely will stop at a level of unvarnished literacy. Usually some educational considerations of style will come to mind. (We will say more about these considerations in the next section of this chapter when we discuss basic competence testing.)

The difference between socializing and educating seems, despite its imprecision, to be a fundamentally important distinction to bear in mind when thinking about the organization of the school curriculum. In making decisions about what should go into the curriculum, we must separate criteria drawn from notions of socializing from criteria drawn from notions of education. It is important to be aware of this distinction and to be aware that while socializing and educational activities are not themselves in conflict in any way, there may well be conflict for curriculum time between the two. Thus someone who seeks a single general criterion for deciding what should go into the curriculum is likely to collapse one into the other. Consequently, appeals to "disciplines" are often appeals that implicitly reject or diminish the importance of socializing criteria in choosing curriculum content; and appeals to "relevance" often implicitly reject educational criteria.

A significant dimension of change in our society over the past half-century has been the increasing influence of socializing criteria in determining what should be done in schools, and the waning influence of educational criteria. The school has been made responsible for an expanding range of socializing activities that previously were considered the proper roles of other social institutions, such as the family. Thus sex education, driving instruction, cooking, and so on, have ferreted their way into the curriculum, and have become the responsibility of schools. If there is a crisis in our schools at present, it seems to us largely due to the schools' acceptance of an ever-increasing role and responsibility in the socialization of the young. It is a set of responsibilities that teachers are inadequately equipped to handle. If teachers have a professional status, it surely lies in the fact that they are trained to be able to educate the young. That professional status must suffer increasing erosion if teachers come to be considered as merely another set of socializing agents within society.

Schools socialize of necessity. They do so incidentally to whatever roles they perform. We are concerned in this book about a series of confusions that arise in the study of education, in the making of curricula, and in teaching practice — confusions that follow from failing to distinguish socializing from educating in any systematic way. Our underlying concern is with the general social results of the retreat of education in the face of the increasing dominance of socializing criteria in deciding the proper purposes of schools.

Many disputes in education follow because people hold different presuppositions about the degree to which schools should socialize and the degree to which they should educate. Thus disputes about "equality of educational opportunities" are not likely to be resolved while some of the disputants are more concerned with what we would call "equality of socializing opportunities," but do not recognize the difference. As long as the distinction remains hidden in an expanded sense of "educating" — an expansion that we will argue below has been influentially encouraged by John Dewey—the dispute can only continue fruitlessly.

Some areas of study that are useful in socialization are mistakenly believed to have value in education—because the two functions are not understood to be different. Under such a heading we would include—as we argue in chapters eight and nine—much of "educational" psychology. It is not insignificant that so much research in the area of "educational" psychology is funded by the military. People who need efficient military "personnel" need to train them to perform particular precise functions. The end product of the training is preordained. This is paradigmatic of socializing. Activities are justified in terms of a precise end, and this end is a function to be performed for some useful purpose distinct from personal cultivation. Education is unlike this, because there is no precise "end" for everyone, nor are learning activities justified on instrumental grounds, nor are they determined in hierarchical sequences according to the dictates of the functions to be performed by the socialized or trained person. If we fail to make a distinction between socializing and educating, the technological models appropriate to the former may become mistakenly applied to the latter. But if we keep the distinction clearly in mind, we may defend ourselves against this elementary confusion.

Let us try to etch the distinction a little more clearly by seeing an example of what happens when we fail to observe it.

BASIC COMPETENCE TESTING

Golda Meir is the president of Egypt, and the United States is a member of the Common Market. The Educational Testing Service reports that 27 percent of all high school seniors believe the first claim, and that 40 percent believe the second. As if this statistic were not bad enough, the National Assessment of Educational Progress tells us that only half the nation's seventeen-year-olds can organize ideas on paper. Most can do no better than a few random sentences.

It seems that about half the students who have gone to high school cannot get ideas sorted out in their heads or in writing. There has been no similar formal testing of their skills in conversation, so far as we know, but our guess is that the art of conversation is not much practiced or even distinguished by many from other sorts of informal verbal encounters that serve to pass the time. After all, how could one hold a sustained exchange of ideas, being careful not to mislay the main point in a bramble of incidentals, pressing together in the same direction, refining points and perceptions until some profitable understanding has been reached, if one's partner in discussion thinks Golda Meir is president of Egypt?

There certainly is talk enough among students and between students and teachers, but too often it is talk of the quick, cagey, headlong kind or the phatic kind. There is pressure to teach phatic usage, that is, speech meant to share or reveal feelings or to arouse feelings rather than to communicate ideas. And we seem to teach the multiple-choice reflex instead of the investigative disposition. Being right — quickly — is valued more often than being able to construct new problems, puzzles, or questions on one's own and then being able to express them with precision.

Quick, cagey, headlong phatic language (and social encounters) characterize teaching and learning in too many schools for our long-term good. It is the main purpose of education to pass along the culture we have, and now we must own up to the educational consequences that follow in a society that has replaced personal written correspondence with printed messages on Hallmark cards and ubiquitous telephone calls. Is there anyone alive among your students and friends whose collected letters would make good reading?

There is no doubt that we have a problem in North America with reading and writing. There is some argument, though, about the sort of problem it is and what a reasonable solution might be. The problem is deeply settled in among us and it has a long history. It is basically a political and moral problem rather than an educational one. And the current zeal for basic competence testing is a premature, false simplification whose temperature at the moment is higher than its promise.

The problem of basic incompetence in high school reading and writing is emphatically not a new problem; neither is it a budding educational or social catastrophe. It is only more shameful and embarrassing now that it has been brought to light again by new studies; and because we spend so much money on the schools, we think we have the right to expect fewer failures from them.

As long as we aim to provide high school facilities and instruction for everyone, and as long as the majority of humankind remains disposed roughly as it has been since literacy became a possibility, we have no grounds for expecting anything greatly different from what has always been and is now the case: most people do not write well or often, if at all; and most people do not read well, even though they may look at pages by the ream. Nowadays it is actually considered rather eccentric and perverse to stoop, sitting still, over colorless pages that do not beat rhythmically, shimmer chromatically, or entice pharmacologically. In a world preoccupied with manufactured entertainments in every medium, what is the attraction of sitting quietly, in private, struggling with the meanings of words and ideas?

Changes in high school programs during the 1970s reflect an answer to this question. In Massachusetts between 1971 and 1976, forty-three high schools showed an increase of 50 percent in the number of English/Language Arts courses offered as electives. But most of these "English" courses covered film, television, and science fiction. Between 1968 and 1973, over 25 percent of Massachusetts high schools added film-making courses, while the number of schools offering eleventh grade English and World History went down. In California between 1971 and 1975, enrollment in basic English courses declined 19 percent, and in English composition it fell 77 percent, while enrollments doubled in electives such as children's theater, the mystery and detective story, and in something called Executive English.

The Advisory Panel on the SAT Score Decline, after considering these data, said:

> Our firmest conclusion is that the critical factors in the relationship between curricular change and the SAT scores are (1) that less thoughtful and critical reading is now being demanded and done, and (2) that careful writing has apparently about gone out of style.[1]

And later in the same report the panel concluded, "We attach central importance to restoring the traditions of critical reading and careful writing." They go on to stipulate that they

> are not suggesting simplistic "solutions" through which all students are treated alike by being held to in a grade until they meet a common standard . . . subjected to the same more demanding reading materials, overloaded with homework, confronted with some national common denominator of college entrance, or denied needed help in skills development in college. . . . The only right answer is to vary the instructional process still more to take account of the increased individual differences, but without lowering standards — which we recognize as a form of magic, but one that has been performed in this country for a long time.[2]

One must not assume that the younger generation is responsible for this semiliterate state of things. It is estimated now that about 40 percent of Americans' leisure time—and an average of one thousand hours per year for the first sixteen years of life — is spent in front of television sets. It is also well documented now that

> a constantly increasing percentage of textbook space is taken up by pictures, larger print, wider margins, shorter words and sentences and paragraphs; the amount of exposition is decreasing, the amount of narrative is going up . . . student testing is being reduced to an "objective answer" basis, meaning that students will find less reason to learn to write: "generally, the assignment in the Reading, History, and Literature textbooks [asks] only for underlining, circling and filling in or single words."[3]

The point being labored here is that the problem of incompetence in reading and writing is a symptom of a more profound problem— that of a whole culture letting literacy lapse under the pressures of simple, monosyllabic messages in lots of white space that everyone is sure to "get" and that give little in the way of appreciation for language mastery or motivation to develop one's skills in reading or writing beyond the conceptual equivalent of a grunt.

Literate and *competent* both have a weak and a strong sense. The weak sense of *literate* is "able to read and write" and a pupil who can pencil out "Jack daddy home" and then say it back out loud would count as literate in the weak sense. The weak sense of *competent* is "answering all requirements: legally qualified," and a pupil who could "pass" four years of high schooling, whatever the standards for passing, would be certified as competent at the high school level.

The strong sense of *competent* is "fitness, capacity, and adequacy," the sense that Chief Justice Warren Burger apparently had in mind when he told the American Bar Association that half the lawyers who appear in American courtrooms are not competent. When this strong sense of competence is applied to the skills of literacy, we find half the students in American classrooms are not competent either.

The strong sense of *literate* is "acquainted with letters and literature; educated, instructed, learned" meaning, at a bare minimum, the ability to recognize and explain what is wrong with saying "Jack daddy home." But it means something even more important. Skills of reading and writing are akin to skills of thinking. We believe Jefferson had this idea in mind when in 1816 he wrote, "If a nation expects to be ignorant and free, in a state of civilization, it expects what never was and what never will be."

Reading and writing are tools for sharpening critical perceptions; that is, they are tools for thinking. Reading is being a critical judge of someone else's thinking and values; writing is the act of becoming a critical judge of one's own thinking and values. Being a critical judge means being able to make and follow a series of conceptual choices. It means knowing the logical relations between evidence and conclusion, between reason and decision, between assertion and justification. These patterns of relationship occur in all writing, not exclusively in analytical writing. They are just as much a part of speculative literature, biography, and journalism; of poetry, prose fiction, and literary criticism; of religious tracts; and of legal and psychological case studies.

Reading and writing in a sense *are* thinking; they reform and refine each other as they inform and define the life of the mind. To learn reading and writing is to learn how to think. It is to confront one's own thoughts by way of confronting the thoughts of others. Such confrontation of one's own thoughts is largely a private matter, while reporting on the results is more public, if it takes the form of writing for others to read, or the even rarer form of structured conversation, which is oral composition done cooperatively. In either case, clear expression is thinking's sternest test.

At present the weak senses of competence and literacy dominate the talk and the forms of basic competence testing in reading and writing. For example, the New York State tests once asked that high school graduates be able to read a recipe for chili pizza well enough to indicate the pan size required and how many persons the dish would accommodate for a meal. Another question asked the student merely to identify prices on a menu, and so it goes. To appreciate the standards assumed for competence and literacy in these tests, one need only know that the tests may be given either on or before entrance to high school; thus an elementary and junior high school curriculum is presumed sufficient for meeting this legal qualification of high school competence. It may be useful socialization, but it is an educational sham.

The reason for this sham is political. It is simply out of the question to base these tests on standards high enough to reflect a strong sense of competence or literacy because about half our high school students could not pass them. As it is, these students graduate anyway, and school officials thus avoid dangerous social and political consequences that would follow exorbitant school failure while they deck out statistically the ideal of equal educational opportunity for all. But the states now want to deny high school certificates to those who cannot pass the basic minimal competence tests because the public clamor about this so-called sudden catastrophe of incompetence makes it seem as though they ought to do something—anything—to maintain respectability.

Some of those who have thought about the consequences of competence testing have had a vision of twenty or so urban centers, mostly non-white, filling up the streets with young men and women who were denied a high school diploma and with it the mandatory qualification for most types of work. This vision is a social and political horror, so down go the standards of competence and up go the numbers of doubtfully certified competent in the high schools. And nothing essentially changes in the way of reading, writing, or thinking abilities, or in the way of literacy in its strong sense. Nothing changes except that the public is mollified for a time on the subject of school accountability.

In a short while these tests will likely serve as instruments for heterogeneous placement in the same fashion as IQ and other achievement tests have done in the past. Then the clamor will shift back to an equalitarian dirge, mournful because we forgot once again that testing does not help when thinking does not count.

When such testing is a legal requirement for high school graduation, another consequence we might anticipate is the vortex effect. A vortex is a mass of fluid having a circular motion tending to form a cavity or vacuum at the center and to draw down into this cavity all those bodies subject to its power. Mass testing for minimal competence, with legal sanctions to enforce it, will draw down to the vacuum of minimal standards all those teaching and learning bodies subject to it. To ask for so little is to expect even less.

Teaching the skills of reading and writing is an undertaking of some moral significance, and to an extent the problem of literacy is a moral problem.

It is evident from the discussion so far that skills in reading and writing are closely related to the skills of critical thinking. It is also the case that self-control, or autonomy, is closely related to critical thinking because to be autonomous means to be governed by one's own reason. This reason, like all other reason, is subject to the standards of good reason, that is, consistency, coherence, relevance, and so on; therefore the quality of one's reasoning will be shaped by one's knowledge of the appropriate standards to use in its development, and this knowledge will determine the quality of one's self-governance. To be governed well by one's own good reason is to be protected against misuse by others who would indoctrinate or dominate one for reasons of their own. To be misused by others in this way is to lose one's autonomy, one's freedom to govern oneself by one's own (good) reason. Insofar as reading and writing skills inform and refine thinking, they also protect one's freedom.

Just as social ethics is normative, so is grammar: it is a prescription of rules for reaching specific goals. The rules of grammar need to be mastered if one is to use the language to reach goals that involve critical thought. As C. S. Peirce put it, "Logic is the ethics of thinking —in the sense in which ethics is the bringing to bear of self-control for the purpose of realizing our desires."[4]

To the extent that schools do not teach skills in reading and writing as the normative grammar of good reason, and to the extent that literacy in the strong sense does not account for the standards of such teaching (and the teachers themselves), and to the extent that phatic usage is the norm for language arts, schools will not produce educated graduates, no matter how many are socialized and certified as minimally competent.

In a democratic political system, identified for its resolute determination to provoke and protect public debate on issues that affect the lives of its citizens, justice will be designed in the words of those who can speak, read, write, and reason with understanding. We cannot expect to be ignorant, or even minimally competent, and free for long.

We surely must prevent our high school graduates from thinking that Golda Meir is president of Egypt, but this will not be done with multiple choice tests on chili pizza or any other politically indulgent, reductionist, basic minimal-competence testing form. A more likely alternative solution to this problem is the reinstitution of critical reading and careful writing, with due regard for individual differences not only in our elementary and secondary schools, but also in the college programs that certify teachers to teach in these schools.

The form of minimal-competence testing may satisfy some who holler at the educators, but the standards these tests purport to guarantee are a mockery of high school education and should fool nobody. This official legitimatization of low standards is less tolerable and more misleading than an admission of the predictable rate of failure to meet higher ones that still have some meaning and deserve some respect.

If our schools accept the proposition that their role is basic socialization only and continue to give certificates of competence on minimal achievements of appropriate skills, they are apparently accepting the second proposition that education will remain an elite process. Equality of *educational* opportunity is not even being attempted or envisioned. We may incorporate the ideal of equality of educational opportunity by the simple expedient of substituting "educational" for "socializing" in "equality of socializing opportunity." If socialization and education are so easily distinguishable, how is it that this substitution is so commonly and subconsciously performed? In North America the great achievement of the public schools has been the creation of a social unit out of diverse groups with diverse traditions. They have socialized well. What has been tenuous in North America is a distinct and clear educational tradition. At the time when one might have expected to see this develop, during the period of rapidly growing affluence early in this century, the influence of John Dewey, among others, helped to suppress what might have been a clearer sense of the distinct educational and socializing roles of the public schools.

THE SOCIALIZATION OF JOHN DEWEY

Much has been written about how far John Dewey's ideas have been misinterpreted and about whether his ideas have ever been adequately put into practice. Whatever we conclude about such things, it is surely clear that North American educational thinking and practice have been influenced by Dewey as by no one else. His influence is significant in the area that this book is about. We believe that his enormous influence has encouraged the advance of socializing within our schools, and the retreat of education.

Dewey distinguishes that kind of education "which everyone gets from living with others"[5] from the kind of education that may result from formal instruction. Also he distinguishes between studies of intrinsic value and those engaged for some instrumental purpose, and he stresses the importance of finding in any study or activity an aesthetic quality that will make it of intrinsic value for the individual. Now while these distinctions reflect something of the distinction made above between socializing and educating, they are also different from it in some important ways.

Dewey would not, of course, use the term socializing as a good label for anything he would distinguish from education. He, and indeed most people, would quite happily include the activities we are calling socializing under a broad sense of education. We have made this distinction in these particular terms to point out that for Dewey what we have called socializing activities are paradigmatic forms of education to which all educational activities ought to conform, and that he tends to use a criterion drawn from what we have called socializing to judge the purposes and appropriate content for education as a whole.

(We are not, of course, trying to argue that our distinction between socializing and educational activities is "true" or in every sense better than Dewey's distinction. We want simply to establish that ours is a sensible distinction and we make it because it helps to clarify some distinct things that Dewey finds unnecessary or unimportant to distinguish in the same way. Our concern, then, is with the implications that follow from Dewey's finding it an unimportant distinction.)

Dewey says: "What nutrition and reproduction are to physiological life, education is to social life."[6] In applying our distinction one would put "socialization" rather than "education" in that sentence. (This is not, of course, to disagree with Dewey, because his use of "education" here clearly incorporates both our notion of education and of socialization. What is significant is that for Dewey no such distinction is considered important.) He adds: "When we have the outcome of the [educational] process in mind, we speak of . . . shaping into the standard form of social activity."[7] He is emphatic that, "With the wide range of possible material to select from, it is important that education . . . should use a criterion of social worth."[8]

Dewey is arguing against a form of education that he sees as belonging to class-divided states, wherein the aristocracy enjoys an "ornamental" classical education of personal cultivation and almost exclusively of intrinsic value, and the lower classes learn instrumental, utilitarian skills. In his democracy, the social experience of democratic life is to ensure that no such division will occur. All studies for everyone are to be both intrinsically valuable and instrumentally useful: "It is the particular task of education at the present time to struggle in behalf of an aim in which social efficiency and personal culture are synonyms instead of antagonists."[9] It may be noted in passing that "synonyms" forms an odd contrast to "antagonists." One might more easily say that social efficiency and personal cultivation should be combined, or be seen as compatible, in any individual. By suggesting that they should be synonymous, Dewey suggests that they should be the same thing; that is, in our terms, socializing and educating should be identical.

The ever-present danger Dewey sees to this democratic aim is that certain kinds of studies will become formal and abstract, and escape from the social experience of democratic life, creating a kind of mandarin mentality in those who follow this path, thus creating again the old social divisiveness. And, of course, "formal education is peculiarly exposed to this danger."[10] This fear of escape from the realities of everyday democratic experience powerfully influences his notion of what should form the content of the curriculum: "The subject matter of education consists primarily of the meanings which supply content to existing social life."[11]

Dewey's conception of social life is not nearly so narrow as is suggested by our notion of socialization. Dewey means much more than the basic social utility we refer to. Our purpose here is not so much to offer an exegesis of Dewey's ideas, nor, in this case, of the influence of people such as G. H. Mead on them, as it is to express a concern with what has happened once these ideas are applied to the curriculum. While we cannot sensibly claim that Dewey was only concerned with what we call socializing, we can nevertheless point out the fact that there is a powerful trend in his writing to make socializing criteria dominant in determining curriculum content and providing purposes for the educational process as a whole. Also, once these ideas have been abstracted from the richness and complexity of meanings and associations in which they exist in Dewey's writings, they take on, in determining curriculum content, a simpler, clearer, and more restrictive sense nearer to our notion of socializing.

The strong tendency of Dewey's thought in the direction of letting socializing criteria dominate education as a whole, may be seen in his vision of the place of Social Studies in the general curriculum. In his attempt to prevent formal studies from being isolated from their social effects and possibilities, he seeks to make Social Studies the center of the curriculum to which all other studies can be tied. So he says, the Social Studies "are so important that they should give direction and organization to all branches of study."[12]

This tendency to see what we have called socializing as the

paradigmatic form of education, and to rein all studies tightly to
social effects and possibilities, seems to involve two major problems
for the curriculum that embodies these ideas, albeit imperfectly and
vaguely.

A first problem might be seen in what becomes of studies such as
history and geography when sucked into a Social Studies curriculum
dominated by criteria drawn from notions of socializing. As Dewey
puts it, "The function of historical and geographical subject matter
. . . is to enrich and liberate the more direct personal contacts of life by
furnishing their context, their background and outlook."[13] That is,
their function is to serve as enrichment factors in the socializing
process. If they have to furnish the context, background, and outlook
of present "personal contacts of life" — if these are to provide the
criteria for choosing which history and geography is most worth
studying — then we get the kind of local, regional, and national
history and geography that are in fact the staple of the secondary
Social Studies curriculum, and that are what we have distinguished
as socializing activities. That is, no distinct criterion is offered to
justify studying history for its own sake, for seeing it as an autonomous mode of inquiry and an autonomous form of knowledge, or for
developing a sophisticated historical consciousness.

Since Dewey sees the function of these distinct forms of knowledge and modes of inquiry as such a present-oriented socializing and
limited one, it is no surprise that he can blend them into one: "While
geography emphasizes the physical side and history the social, these
are only emphases in a common topic, namely, the associated life of
man."[14] They are thus simply "two phases of the same living
whole."[15]

Similarly, Dewey recommends study of Indian life in North
America because our present solutions to the social problems of
providing shelter, food, protection, and so on are so complex.

> Recourse to the primitive may furnish the fundamental elements of
> the present situation in immensely simplified form. It is like un-
> raveling a cloth so complex and close to the eyes that its scheme
> cannot be seen, until the larger coarser features of the pattern appear
> . . . and by seeing how these were solved in the earlier days of the
> human race, form some conception of the long road which has had
> to be traveled, and of the successive inventions by which the race
> has been brought forward in culture.[16]

So also industrial history is to be studied because it "reveals the
successive causes of social progress."[17] This emphasis on society,

which is supposed to make studies interesting because they are real to children's experience, means that a focus on heroes or great people runs a great danger of isolating the doings of such heroes from their "social situations . . . from the conditions that aroused [them] and to which [their] activities were a response."[18] For similar reasons Dewey claims that "Economic history is more human, more democratic, and hence more liberating than political history."[19] (These seem to be cases where Dewey's "psychological principle" — what children naturally find interesting — comes into conflict with his socializing purpose. It seems that in such cases the former must give way to the latter.)

Dewey's ideas about the proper role of history and geography in the curriculum seem to be commonly reflected in much simpler terms in typical Social Studies textbooks, where one sees history and geography described as extensions of present experience in time and space, or some such. The fact that one is an empirical science and the other a study of past human events reconstructed from present traces, having different kinds of methodologies, theories, and modes of expression, does not prevent their being taken as twin extensions out from the present.

Our concern, then, is to trace some results of what seems to us a diminishing concern with — even the collapse of — education in the face of demands for socializing. The results seem often to be insidious and quite unnoticed by many promoting them. We will argue, to take one example mentioned above, that the huge enterprise of educational psychology is very largely a promoter of socializing practices and is so insensitive to distinctions between socializing and educating that it is contributing to the destruction of the latter. We will argue, for example, that an inability to distinguish properly between instructing and teaching and the consequent recommendation that findings about the former be incorporated in definitions of the latter act to undermine education.

CONCLUSION

Many disputes about the curriculum can be greatly helped, if not resolved, by observing this distinction between educating and socializing. Disputes about who should decide what goes into the curriculum, for example, may be helped. Observing that social and political officials have not only a right but a duty to specify core curricula as far as socialization is concerned and that educated people need to be consulted about the construction of educational curricula immediately takes us a long way. It might not take us all the way — it does not solve completely the question of what belongs under educating and what under socializing and it leaves the overlapping area in dispute— but it may help us avoid the silliness of committees of parents, politicians, and administrators deciding on an educational curriculum and the silliness of educators claiming special authority in matters of socialization.

The distinction also may help teachers in defining their professional role. At present they seem professionally helpless against ever-increasing demands that they serve as the administrators of a social catch-all institution which is becoming so absorbed in various socialization functions that it has little time and less energy left for education. This simple distinction might give teachers' organizations a better means of defining their unique professional status as educators, and consequently a means of clearly marking out what socializing tasks are not their responsibility, nor that of the schools. Other institutions could serve many of the socializing needs that at present are pushing education out of our schools. We think it is time to push education back into our classrooms and time, perhaps, to plan for other institutions to handle many of the socializing activities that have come to replace education.

CHAPTER TWO

The Socialization of Schools

STUDYING THE WORTH and purpose of education is both hard and easy. It is hard because we are not able to achieve what any of us would consider adequate control of all the essential concepts. It is easy because so many people have something useful and insightful to add that, collectively, we make considerable gains on our ignorance, even though as individuals we may contribute only a little. In any case, we are better off as communities, and as a society, for setting ourselves to the work of examining the meanings education has and should have, for to do such work is to learn more about the reasons for being the way we are, and about our chances of becoming what we wish to be.

There is a temptation (a regressive, seductive nostalgia is perhaps more like it) that entices us toward resolution, conclusion, and simplicity when we think about educational issues and concepts. We are not yet ready to agree with Russell that the demand for certainty, though perfectly natural, is an intellectual vice; but we are steered by Burckhardt's warning that ours would be an age of great simplifiers, tending away from complexity and toward tyranny. We feel this tendency sometimes in our own work, and it is apparent in the literature of education to a degree that is a challenge to our powers of justification.[1] But the problem is not only an educational one. Fifty years ago Justice Benjamin Cardozo wrote of the certainty that is genuine and the certainty that is illusory in the law, and he saw that "overemphasis of certainty may carry us to the worship of an intolerable rigidity," and that even if "we were to state the law today as well as human minds can state it, new problems, arising almost overnight, would encumber the ground again."[2]

We can continue to refine the logic of the law and the logic of our philosophies of education until we reach a certain point. At that point

17

we face divergence and dilemma, choices that must be made by judges and by educators not on the strength of the law itself and not on the implications of philosophy alone. At that point, judges and educators are rescued not only by logic, but by something closer to aesthetics—a sense of history, culture, custom, or a principle of social responsibility that provides confidence in evaluation and in long-term visions—or by "some compelling sentiment of justice or sometimes perhaps a semi-intuitive apprehension of the pervading spirit of our law."[3]

These are the beliefs we hold most strongly; they are close to the core of what we call "character" in human personality; they are the primitive terms by which we generate and measure reason itself. They are the characteristics of what we mean by education.

Education and law can never be analyzed completely; nor can logic alone give a satisfactory answer to the most fundamental questions raised as to their nature and purpose. However, by exploring the ways they might serve each other by analogy, common metaphor, and rules of precedent, some educational issues of serious national concern may at least be set more clearly for debate.

EDUCATIONAL POLICY AND LAW

In the last fifteen or twenty years there has been a Gargantuan swiveling of the law. If Nathan Glazer is right, the turning is irreversible.[4] Whereas the tradition of law in Anglo-Saxon countries has been to concentrate on the protection of property and the limitation of governmental power, the turning has showed us a new, expanded power of the law, which now comes to include most critical social services—from housing and medical care to public schooling. This expansion is not simply an enlargement of the area of civic life that falls under the legal purview; it is a change in kind for the issues and policies that now concern the law. More precisely, the question of legal rights is no longer the only or even the primary concern in cases dealing with education; the result of the judgment on rights is in effect the beginning of a social policy. A judicial decision, however, is not sufficient for outlining a policy; nor is it often of much use at all in developing the prudent connection between knowledge and power.

Developing this prudent connection between knowledge and power is the activity of normative policy-making. Educational policy-makers do this within a broad but special intellectual context that is called a "conception of education." Normative problems, those needs that require and justify policies, are themselves conceived in terms and categories limited by the provisions of a given conception of education. A conundrum in one conception is a virtue in another, just as a basic principle in one may be a mystery in another. If one sees that the nature of a given conception of education has a profound and inevitable effect on the generation of policy, then the importance of analyzing the conception of education that embodies policy becomes clear. What is not so clear to many of us is how to go about such analysis, and how to develop new conceptions to replace the ones we are using when the latter are found to be inadequate.

If judicial decisions are in fact the beginnings of social policy, and if judicial decisions in matters of public education are the beginnings of educational policy, then it seems worth our while to discover, if we can, what conception of education is providing the basic principles by which such decisions, and later, policies, are being made.

CONCEPTIONS, FACTS, AND EDUCATIONAL POLICY

Why analyze conceptions of education if the focus of these decisions and subsequent policies is on the practical problems of public schooling? Some would argue that the analysis of conceptions of education is a weak response to the social, political, and economic problems we have to face in the context of public schooling. These people would argue that the examination of facts is more to the point than discussions of theory, or even worse, philosophy. They would argue, for example, that if some index of achievement showed that students of an informal classroom do less well than those of a more traditional classroom, or if the index showed predominantly black-segregated schools do less well than white-segregated ones, then the informal classroom and the black-segregated school should be eliminated, if the results of such an index are educationally significant. This primeval policy inference is not justified on the proposed facts of the case any more than its opposite—directing that more money be spent precisely according to areas where the index of achievement is low (lowest)—would be justified. Of course both policies are justifiable, if the conceptions of education that they are meant to serve are specified and properly located in the legal, political, social, and philosophical context that provides each its rationale. The simple consideration of conceptually forsaken fact will not do for making policy.

This type of argument, however compelling for its interest in immediate action and its pragmatic vocabulary, is predicated on a belief that facts can be considered as simple units, like stones. This belief is both fallacious and tyrannous in its simplicity. Dewey called it the "neglect of context" fallacy, the analytic form of which is found "whenever the distinctions of elements that are discriminated are treated as if they were final and self-sufficient."[5] Those contented with possessing or gathering facts only are not so much liable to a charge of ignorance as they are likely to be stupid, in Gilbert Ryle's sense of the difference. "Stupidity is not the same thing, or the same sort of thing, as ignorance. There is no incompatibility between being well informed and being silly, and a person who has a good nose for argument or jokes may have a bad head for facts."[6] Whereas good and profitable argument can be carried on in relative ignorance, that is to say, in the absence of many "facts," it should be clear that stupidity cannot be overcome with any conceivable number of simple "fact units."

It is especially important for policy-makers to recognize the point being made here about the conceptual bed in which facts must lie; otherwise they are likely to draw the tempting but illogical conclusion that if only enough data were at hand, then the "best" policy could be derived from them. There is a fallacy in this thinking: descriptive, factual statements cannot provide us with the logical force to make decisions about what we or others ought to do. These decisions can be made with or without copious data, as indeed they are most of the time. But they cannot even be imagined in the absence of certain held beliefs about what is good, what is right, and what we want. These beliefs are essential to making decisions of an ethical nature, that is, decisions about what we and others ought to do. It follows that these beliefs are essential to making educational policy decisions, because such decisions always prescribe what those involved in education ought to do.

Another example of this point may be found in the common practice of tracking students on the basis of IQ scores and selected aptitude test scores. It is true that such tests produce data about gross similarities and differences within certain groups. However, the decision to group students on the basis of these data, and not on some other basis, is made on independent and value-laden grounds. Teachers may think that *efficiency* is better served by aptitude and achievement grouping. Here the value is "efficiency in teaching." Other teachers, with as much and perhaps more justification, may think that the cost in negative social learning far exceeds the gain in efficient academic teaching, and would choose therefore to group students heterogeneously using the same data as the teachers who would group homogeneously.

This argument helps us realize that values, in the form of held beliefs, are essential to policy-making in education, whereas facts are not. Similarly, insofar as a legal decision becomes law, it becomes fact, but not until it becomes a held value does it become effective for influencing educational policy. The common example of this relation between the fact of a judicial decision and the values that determine educational policy is the twenty-odd year lacuna after *Brown v. Board of Education*.[7] Those who were in sympathy with the civil rights concerns of the Warren Court cheered the decision as *evidence* that the Constitution was showing its strength and justice against repressive odds. Those who viewed the Constitution and the Warren Court as ineluctable enemies saw the Brown decision as *evidence* that the Constitution was being unjustly used. The "fact" of that decision was subverted by the values of those who disagreed with it in communities all over the country. In this subversion one can see that the power of fact, even so grand a "fact" as a constitutional law come into existence by edict of the Supreme Court, is no match for the power of value-beliefs that determine our conceptions. It is the conception that gives the fact its value more often than the fact that changes a conception. George Kelly's psychology of personal constructs and Thomas Kuhn's philosophy of scientific revolutions testify convincingly to this point.[8]

FIVE FAMILIAR CONCEPTIONS OF "EDUCATION" AND AN ALTERNATIVE

The conceptions of education that have provided Western civilization with its pedagogical principles and related social policies are few—surprisingly few when considered in the context of intellectual development generally. We would like to give a brief synoptic description of the major conceptions that we have been able to identify, and then to propose an alternative one that uses the distinction between education and socialization that we are trying to emphasize.

The first four of these conceptions are epistemologically oriented, and very much concerned with individual processes of learning. The fifth shifts back and forth between the process and the

product sense of education, emphasizing the latter in terms of the
social organization of schools.

Education as Insight

The governing metaphor in this conception of education is
Plato's cave allegory,[9] which has served as our image of enlightenment, whether secular or religious, for over two thousand years. The
allegory presents the simple and gloomy image of prisoners in a cave,
chained so they can see only passing shadows on a dark wall, cast
from a fire burning outside the cave's mouth. One prisoner frees
himself, sees the cause of the images—the light that casts them—and
crawls through the opening to see not only the fire but the sun. He is
shaken and nearly blinded by his brilliant discovery, but he adjusts to
its profundity and perfection. He would stay in this realm of pure
revelation forever, except for the obligation to return to the others
who have seen no source for the shadows that are their reality. Of
course, they resist the message that their lives are contained in dark
deception, and they would like to kill this self-proclaimed enlightened one, who nevertheless dedicates himself to their instruction. To the extent that being educated and being enlightened have
anything in common, this metaphor brings them together. Knowledge, in this view, as modified by St. Augustine in his revealing
dialogue "The Teacher," is a matter of complete vision — internal
vision that comes more or less naturally when one is in the proper
disposition to *receive* it. No teacher can *provide* knowledge or insight; the teacher can only prompt the student to seek realities not
already known to him. One can see a modern advocate of this concept
of teaching in Carl Rogers. There is in fact a remarkable similarity
between the Augustinian prompter and the Rogerian facilitator: both
assume that really important knowledge (though the two would describe this quite differently) cannot be directly communicated but
that one can prompt or facilitate a search for it. A successful search
culminates in a sort of conversion, a change of belief-with-conviction
that becomes a change in character. Character education of this sort is
predicated on the most conservative and impregnable concept of
knowledge for Augustine; there is no recourse to argument, deliberation, or consideration of evidence with the intention of creating or
changing knowledge. One does not come to have knowledge by
accumulating it in verbal bits and chunks. One prepares for insight,
and for getting knowledge, by developing one's character and receptive disposition.

Education as Impression

John Locke provided us with the model for this conception of education in his striking idea that the human mind is a storage place for external impressions, sifted through the senses, and accumulated in standardizable ways. In this view, the mind becomes raw material for those who would structure learning environments so as to control and to shape mental behavior. It is not altogether reckless to suggest that the modern behaviorist has taken the simplest possible reading of Locke's empiricist propaedeutics and failed to improve on them. Recall John Watson's confident promise that he could guarantee, given a free hand in controlling a child's environment and training, to take any normal infant "and train him to become any type of specialist [he] might select — doctor, lawyer, artist, merchant-chief and, yes, even beggar-man and thief, regardless of his talents, penchants, tendencies, abilities, vocations and race of his ancestors."[10]

This conception of the growth of knowledge does not take into account any significant part for the learner to play; it does not allow for any radical innovation by the learner, nor does it seem to recognize that knowledge is embodied in language, custom, and culture that in the main part is not *controlled* by anybody in particular. The education of B. F. Skinner's *Walden Two* is indebted to this conception.

Education as Growth

The growth metaphor has had an extended and familiar history in educational thought; it can be found serving the purposes of Aristotle, Quintilian, Luther, Montaigne, Rousseau, Froebel, and Dewey,[11] although there is wide variance among these purposes. It was Rousseau, Froebel, and primarily Dewey who made the metaphor into a conception of education. Dewey wrote: "Our net conclusion is that life is development, and that developing, growing, is life. Translated into its educational equivalents, that means (i) that the educational process has no end beyond itself; it is its own end; and that (ii) the educational process is one of continual reorganizing, reconstructing, transforming."[12] The stress here is on procedures of problem-solving and the practical necessity of education rather than its dignity; and since the educational process is its own end, it cannot guide or judge the goodness of its own results. Merely that developing, growing, living, continue is all we may ask of "education." In some ways this conception is similar to the insight model, though of course it lacks the teleology and discipline of the latter, and because of this it tends to be more of a conception of socialization than of education insofar as *any kind* of growing counts.

Education as Rational Autonomy

Rational autonomy is the educational attainment designed by Kant and cherished with public eloquence in our time by Israel Scheffler and R. S. Peters. Peters has blown together the principles of rational autonomy with an even stronger line of cultural transmission in a conception he calls "education as initiation."[13] Scheffler has developed the Kantian ideal straightforwardly into a view of teaching he calls the "rule model."[14]

> For Kant, the primary philosophical emphasis is on reason, and reason is always a matter of abiding by general rules or principles. Reason stands always in contrast with inconsistency and with expediency, in the judgment of particular issues. In the cognitive realm, reason is a kind of justice to the evidence, a fair treatment of the merits of the case, in the interests of truth. In the moral realm, reason is action on principle, action that therefore does not bend with the wind, nor lean to the side of advantage or power out of weakness or self-interest. Whether in the cognitive or the moral realm, reason is always a matter of treating equal reasons equally, and of judging the issues in light of general principles to which one has bound oneself.[15]

The burden of teaching in this conception is developing dignity through principled thought and action, and the highest end is the autonomy of the student's judgment, which is as well and fairly informed as possible.

"Education" as Socialization

This fifth conception of "education" is different from the other four, both because it emphasizes the product sense of education determined by the social structure of schools and because it comes not only from philosophers but from a Supreme Court opinion.

By way of introducing the conception, we would like to recall the process/product distinction alluded to above.

> 'Tis education forms the common mind:
> Just as the twig is bent the tree's inclined.[16]

Alexander Pope's couplet shows how *education* is an ambiguous term, like many others ending in "ion" (e.g., *destruction, erection, selection*). Pope used *education* to mean a process in the first line, a "forming" of the common mind; however, in the second line, *education* is connoted as a product, a fixed inclination. This shift of meaning is common in educational discourse about "getting an education," or "providing educational opportunities."

The single best-known paragraph in the *Brown* v. *Board of Education* opinion, the one that sets out the Supreme Court's conception of education as socialization, is a perfect example of this type of equivocal ambiguity:

> Today, education is perhaps the most important function of state and local governments. Compulsory school attendance laws and the great expenditures for education both demonstrate our recognition of the importance of education to our democratic society. It is required in the performance of our most basic public responsibilities, even service in the armed forces. It is a very foundation of good citizenship. Today it is a principal instrument in awakening the child to cultural values, in preparing him for later professional training, and in helping him to adjust normally to his environment. In these days, it is doubtful that any child may reasonably be expected to succeed in life if he is denied the opportunity of an education. Such an opportunity, where the state has undertaken to provide it, is a right which must be made available to all on equal terms.[17]

Education is referred to in this passage as (1) a function of the government, (2) a requirement for performing basic public responsibilities, (3) a foundation of good citizenship, and (4) an instrument for awakening the child to cultural values. The court thinks more highly than clearly about education. Nevertheless, there is an implicit conception of education that plaits these process/product meanings, however loosely. The conception is one of socialization, another of those "-ion" words that can be ambiguous itself.

The sentence in *Brown* that points most directly at this conception reads: "Today [education] is a principal instrument in awakening the child to cultural values, in preparing him for later professional training, and in helping him to adjust normally to his environment." Here the role of the educational institution is seen to be one of society's instruments for imposing its rules of behavior and its priorities on its children. The only way that a child will be able to "fit in" is by having access to public school systems. This conception of the American public school system as an instrument of socialization is one quite consistent with its historical image. However, the court's analysis does not direct one to identify and articulate the range of values that it considers to be most important in the operation of the educational system. It does not suggest how to relate the concepts of social and educational systems to a conception of *process* of education. Nor does it provide a set of criteria with which to evaluate the process of socialization identified *as* education in the court's decision. This model of education as socialization sets no limits on the procedures to be used in the process of delivering acculturation to students.

The court has equivocated by slipping back and forth between education as a socialized product or result (success in life) and education as the process of "awakening the child to cultural values" without providing any rationale for linking these two senses. The effect of this ambiguity has been a failure in legal remedy, and educational policy that still fails to provide reliable guiding light in the black box of our school socialization system.

We would maintain that the court's conception of education in *Brown* and in later decisions has been one of the product sense of socialization primarily and that this product sense is bound to occupational opportunity not exclusively, but for the most part. It should be clear by now that we do not consider this to be a conception of education at all, but a conception of socialization. Even as such it has some problems of internal coherence and of practical applicability. This conception cannot be forced to meet the requirements of a conception of education, but it can be made into a clearer and more feasible conception of socialization. That is the purpose of the next section. As we said earlier, we do not consider socialization to be an inferior or deficient form of education, but a *different matter* with regard to specific purposes.

An Alternative: Socialization as Community Expression

The central proposition of this conception is that public schooling is and should be a functioning description of the community that delivers its children and pays the teachers. *Schools are mediating agencies maintained by communities for the purpose of transforming childhood into participative adulthood. The historical and social functions of a school express a method by which individuals become communities, and through which these communities describe themselves.* In this view a conception of socialization is more to the point when considering schools in the light of social and legal policy.

It should be pointed out that the community focus of this conception falls in the range between "individuals" and "society." The insight, impression, growth, and rational autonomy conceptions are individually concerned almost to the exclusion of social issues (the exception would be Dewey's version of the growth conception whose focus was strongly social). The socialization conception is, of course, socially concerned. In this last conception, however, the community is introduced as the primary schooling unit. By community we mean a relatively small group of people, adults and children, who would probably be lost in a discussion of "society," and who have at least a school in common among them. It is proposed that schools do and should describe these communities rather than certain individuals only, or the oligarchic society at large.

As such, schools are inherently constraining, and they regiment against certain behavior. Contrary to the argument offered by the advocates of deschooling,[18] however, it does not follow from the fact that schools are constraining that they are innately anti-individual or repressive. Communities will be more or less repressive as they choose, and schools will reflect this choice. This does not mean that all schooling is repressive, *ipso facto*, any more than it means all other forms of community expression are repressive simply by virtue of their being expressive. It is difficult to conceive a form of expression that would not require some sort of constraint for its coherence and transmission: all of us blurting simultaneously anything at all may well be unconstrained, but it is not clearly an example of expression that has any significance in a discussion of education or socialization.

When schooling is understood as a functioning description of a given community and as the processing of childhood into adulthood, then the community must look to its own members when the schools appear repressive. More than sixty years ago Robert Michels told us of the "iron law of oligarchy" and what it means for any naive conception of democracy.[19] It may be of some usefulness to consider his theory in the context of a school community, although it was formulated on the social class level. Briefly, the law states that society cannot exist without a dominant class, and that oligarchy is a sort of preordained form of the common life of great social aggregates. The cause of this oligarchic tiering is to be found in the technical indispensability of leadership and the bureaucratic requirements of dispensing social wealth on a large scale. His logic led him from these premises to deny the possibility of a state without classes. It should be noted that Michels believed in the principles of democracy even though he did not think they could ever be realized; he thought of democracy less as a goal than as an ideal that should be pursued, the net effect of which would be to keep societies and social movements from becoming more oligarchical than they must necessarily be.

By analogy, one could suggest that a school community cannot exist without a dominant group, again because of the technical indispensability of leadership and the bureaucratic requirements of dispensing resources. To the extent that those who lead and control the distribution of resources are repressive, the school community will feel repressed by the school. However, whereas constraint is an inevitable characteristic of oligarchic structure, repression is not. It is the pursuit of democratic ideals within the community that will control the degree of constraint to be allowed, and protect against the intolerable outcome of outright repression.

The question of who shall be the dominant group in a community is different from the same question asked of society. The community orientation limits the context in which leadership, distribution, and dominance come to be defined and managed by the members affected. If it is the case that the school can and does describe the community that supports it, then by examining the school one can learn much about the community. But it does not follow from this, as progressive courts and educators have sometimes assumed, that a change in the school will produce a change in the community, or in society at large. One does not change the object of a description by changing the description; in the same sense one does not stand much of a chance of changing a community by changing the school supported by it. A schooling change will be resisted in a community thoroughly, even violently, when it is seen as a false description.

This conception of schooling as community expression with a degree of inevitable oligarchy reverses the progressive and social reconstructionist views of education as the engine of social change. In this proposed conception, schools reflect descriptively, after the fact, what the communities that support them are like. If the community changes, then the school changes eventually to reflect a new description. It is implied here that when schools are perceived as unsatisfactory, the community must not blame the schools first; nor should the community or benevolent outsiders assume that changing schools will solve the problem. When it is remembered that schools are mediating agencies maintained by a community and that the school is an expression of a method by which individuals become communities, and through which these communities describe themselves, then it becomes clear that problems in the school reflect problems in the community. The solution to the problem in the school lies in the community more than in the school itself. Interracial fighting is not basically a school problem. Lack of sensible discipline or too much insensitive discipline are not primarily school problems. The humiliating desecration of literature, philosophy, and the humanistic studies in general that we are forced to endure in the media, in our "educational" institutions, in our lives daily and relentlessly is not only a school problem. These problems, when they occur in schools, are reflections of the communities that support them.

We do not wish to suggest that there is no reciprocal nature to the relations between school and community, for the school does have some influence on the community. What we do wish to emphasize is that most of the influence comes from — and should come from — the community to shape the school, as a mediating agency between childhood and participative adulthood and as a method by which individuals become communities. If the school introduces a change that is not perceived by the community as an accurate description of its held values, the change will be rejected until and unless the community changes its own view of itself. However, when the community demands a change in the school, or even when the community is changing in an unplanned way, the school in most cases must reflect the change.

There are two significant difficulties with this conception of schooling as community expression. The first is that it is very hard to convince any community that in order to solve its socialization problems it will have to revise itself. After all, socialization is the process that describes what the community is already, and what it expects of its prospective members.

This difficulty is no more than a reflection of democracy's greatest flaw. Although participation is required and protected by the system, it cannot be enforced. It is estimated that fewer than half the eligible voters in this nation participate in its most important elections. What evidence have we that a community will take the care and time necessary to revise itself, even when such revision is clearly implied by the public description of the community that is its schools? A companion issue is the necessity of accepting an unrevised community for what it is, as we must accept individuals for what they are, so long as laws are not broken. The Amish of Wisconsin convinced the Supreme Court that their community deserved to be exempted from state compulsory education law enforcement because to comply would have threatened the continued existence of their community.[20] Chief Justice Burger had little trouble with the Amish community because they were strictly "religious," in a quaintly outmoded sense of that term, and carefully law-abiding in all other regards. The question comes up from this case, however, as to what the criteria might be for constitutional protection, for the very legal legitimacy of other communities whose existence is predicated on philosophical views and personal values, rather than on an eighteenth-century agrarian and religious orthodoxy. If such communities do have claim to legal legitimacy, then it would seem consistent for them to claim the corollary right to express themselves as they see fit, and part of this expression, an essential part, is the schools. This is a renewed argument for pluralism in the public schools.

The second difficulty is that of defining *community* so as to make educational, sociological, and legal sense. We cannot propose a complete and satisfactory definition here, but we do believe that it is possible to develop one, given the necessary cooperation among educators, social scientists, and jurists. The community idea could develop along familiar lines of political, philosophical, religious, ethnic, or geographic unities. No one of these criteria is obviously the best or only one for developing communities; they all can be justified.

In sorting out a definition of community, we must ask when it is that "people define themselves as having important characteristics in common, and when do these become bases for communal identity and action."[21] Communities are social constructions that are created by a consciousness of membership that has in it a sense of common, or shared histories, language, and ethical perspective on conduct. Sharing a common territory is a part of this construction, but not an essential part.

American society is less a rigid stratification of classes, or a geography of neighborhoods, than a topography of pluralist clusters. Americans are divided now more than ever into groups that transcend traditional class and race distinctions. It matters now, and it matters a good deal, how individuals define themselves in terms that include ethnicity, occupation, education, political and organizational affiliation, and so on. Establishing group differences and the grounds for their legitimate standing as communities within society as a whole is a norm in American culture that is replacing the more conservative and traditional norm of acculturation. As Gusfield has put it, "Communal consciousness emerges in the perception and recognition that 'we' have a different set of obligations and rights when acting toward those who are seen as part of 'our' community than toward those who are seen as outside that community."[22]

The important point is that a consciousness of communal membership makes it possible to share with others "a sense of participating in the same history."[23] This perception is more important than class identification or geographical location.

Other ideas may be important, too. One is the collective ability to pay for education, socialization, and other essential social services, an ability that can be regulated by legal means suggested in *Serrano v. Priest*,[24] but not limited to these, when the just distribution of resources has been jeopardized. A school community always ought to have adequate resources for adequate schools. Another idea that we think should be considered is including all generations, parents and nonparents, in the essential structure of the community, and therefore in the reflection of that community that is the school. The separating of generations in a community, the exclusion of older people from the process of schooling, and the strict age segregation of students all contribute to our difficulties in socialization generally, and moral education in particular. Students, early in their school careers, are organized on strict age-grouping schedules, so the way they learn the culture and customs of their community, the way values are tested, is by peer evaluation. Often the resulting moral immaturity of these students, and of our citizens as the students become adults, is shocking. We deserve the shock, but we should not be surprised, given the way we have left values to be learned by students from other students no wiser than themselves.

The size of the unit is important, too, given the iron law of oligarchy. It would seem likely that submunicipal units with significant autonomy and a responsibility for participative democracy as the governing ideal would be optimal.

The prediction here is that school reorganization is going to be the result of a community that has taken for itself new values and has chosen to describe itself in these new terms. Attempts to change the schools first and the community next, if at all, are a little too much like the wish of Dorian Gray that his portrait and not he would grow old. One can only hope that the results will not be so violent and catastrophic as were his.

LIBERALISM, SCHOOLS, AND THE LAW

The conception of school socialization presented here is partially based on the view that liberalism is properly conceived as a perpetual *goal* in democratic process. We take liberalism to be more of a goal than a given style of government or body of doctrine. Liberalism is a term we use to reflect the degree to which individuals, small groups of individuals, and their schools are given sanctity in social milieux mainly made up of large organizations and enduring institutions.

Liberalism is the ideal of achieving respect and protection for those individuals and communities who deserve respect and need protection against the monolithic shadows of organization.

As Summerfield has put it:

> If the goal of individualism is cherished, the institutional delivery system for education will be less like that of the past, when it was designed to adapt individuals to industrial roles, and should become increasingly flexible and adaptive to individual personal development. This would seem to require myriad educational policies depending upon local and small group circumstances (pluralism) and individual need, and seems directly opposite of what can be expected from large-scale federal involvement in educational policy.[25]

Insofar as we can agree with Nathan Glazer's observations, referred to earlier, that a judicial decision on rights is in effect the beginning of a social policy, and insofar as we can accept this view of liberalism and individualism as a goal that for its realization requires just the opposite of large-scale federal involvement, then our logic leads us to be skeptical of the expanding role of the courts in making decisions as to the conduct of public education and the policies that guide it.

Our skepticism extends beyond the courts to the politicians and civil servants who serve the federal government. Over the last twenty-five years their presence in the classrooms of North America has increased greatly, beginning in the early 1950s with the chartering of the National Science Foundation to improve science and science education in U.S. schools, and a little later with the National Defense Education Act which specified curriculum emphases in both secondary and elementary schools. Education — at least schooling — had gone national as a political issue, and the federal government had overcome the constitutional tradition of its separation from public school policy-making and state autonomy with regard to education. Schools were viewed as instruments for achieving a new standard of national defense — as instruments of socialization — by the government in Washington.

Since then, through such legislation as the Elementary and Secondary Education Act and the Education of All Handicapped Children Act and through such federally supported projects as the NSF program called "Man — A Course of Study" (MACOS), the federal government has become involved with the *details* of teaching, testing, and curriculum planning to a degree that would have been unimaginable before Eisenhower became president.

Politicians at the state level have come into the schools, too, through many doors opened by legislation. What goes on in classrooms—with whom, for whom, and for its duration—is regulated to an alarming extent by mandates covering teacher performance evaluation, minimum-competence testing, special education for the handicapped, the gifted, and the non-native English speaking, vocational, health, alcohol- and drug-abuse "education," and some specified number of minutes of "the arts" each week.[26]

It becomes ever more difficult for communities to see themselves reflected in their own schools, crowded as they are with federal and state officials who bring *their* ideas about socialization into the classroom. We wonder where, in such a busy place, an educator could fit in long enough to teach.

CHAPTER THREE

The Need for Educational Theory

THE FORM TOWARD WHICH the socialization process is to move is evident—if sometimes contentious—in the form of the society in which the students are to become agents. There may be disputes about which knowledge, skills, and attitudes are more "relevant" for proper preparation to perpetuate the society, but such arguments may be engaged by comparing the relative values of the competing knowledge, skills, and attitudes for the particular society that exists. If our concern is the transformation of society, we begin to introduce ideals that take us beyond matters of socialization and into matters of education. No longer, that is, are we able to justify activities according to a criterion of social utility, but we have to justify them according to a more problematic criterion of human value, which will involve, among other things, what we might casually call a theory of human nature.

A socializing theory would thus be concerned with how best to prepare a child to become an effective agent within a particular society. When it comes to socializing, we do not engage in philosophical speculation about the value of the particular society; that is taken—for socializing purposes—as a given. The task is to enable the child to become an effective adult within that given social context. So our socializing theory will have its *telos* established in the beginning. Our ability to analyze societies, of course, is not so well developed that that *telos* will be absolutely precise and unambiguous or free of contention. It will, however, be a source of fairly widespread agreement about what knowledge, skills, and attitudes are required to become an effective agent within it. In certain aboriginal tribes, the skills whereby life is supported would be fairly unambiguous; in Western industrial societies, literacy and some understanding of democratic political processes would be readily agreed on as prerequisite to effective citizenship. That someone might call for a trans-formation of society which might change or eliminate the need for these particular skills is irrelevant to the socializing theory. Such transformations simply redefine what some future socializing theory will contain. That is to say that such a theory to be useful must be society bound.

If our *telos* is given — that is, for the present society — it also provides the criterion for judging the appropriateness of the particular content of the socializing curriculum. The task then is to ensure efficient instruction so that curriculum is learned as well as possible. And for this we may turn for help to psychological theories of instruction, learning, development, and motivation.

What is sketched in the previous paragraph is, in very general terms, much the form in which it seems commonly supposed an educational theory might be composed; that is, we have an end product established—an image of the ideally educated person—and we then fill out the curriculum content that will achieve that *telos*, and articulate that content within a curriculum to whose design psychological theories of development will contribute and to whose teaching psychological theories of instruction, learning, and motivation will contribute. Educational research, in this view, might then focus on those psychological theories of instruction, learning, motivation, and development and assume that any findings could be applied to, or have implications for, the process of education. This way of thinking about educational research and educational theories is an example of the failure to distinguish between educating and socialization. In this chapter some of the differences between educating and socializing are explored by considering ways in which we might expect educational theories to be different from socializing theories.

THE END PRODUCT

Perhaps the most crucial differences between educating and socializing, and consequently between a useful educational theory and a useful socializing theory, follow from the fact that the end, the *telos*, of the socializing process is relatively precise compared with that of the educational process. The *telos* of the socializing process is a social agent; the *telos* of the educational process is a kind of person. Social utility calls for a social agent familiar with, say, how to vote and what the political groupings stand for. Education calls for a

political philosophy. The constituents of properly socialized agents
are the same. We can specify the necessary knowledge and skills that
are required for anyone to become an effective social agent. The
constituents of every educated person are different. We cannot specify *necessary* ingredients for the educational curriculum. Someone
can be educated and lack any particular piece of knowledge or skill or
attitude that can be specified. Someone could be educated while
lacking necessary socializing knowledge. Such a person might be
eccentric, but eccentricity—a lack of some element considered necessary for proper socialization — is no hindrance to being educated.

To be useful an educational theory should tell us what to teach,
when to teach those things, and how to teach them, and tell us what
we might reasonably expect from so doing. For the "when" and
"how," educators have usually sought implications from psychological theories of development such as Piaget's and theories of instruction such as those discussed in chapter eight. The problem of
specifying the end product of an educational process, however, gives
sharpest point to differences between what we might expect to find in
educational and socializing theories. Superficially it might seem as
though they will be similar, if not the same. Both will answer our
questions about *what*, *when*, and *how* to teach and tell us what our
end product will look like.

Many educational programs have indeed tried to derive their
goals from Piaget's psychological theory. Thus they have tried to
make the curriculum an instrument that aims to further Piaget's
image of the developmental process. ("The ideal of education is . . . to
learn to develop";[1] the purpose of educational institutions is "to lead
children towards intellectual development," as described in Piaget's
theory.[2]) The developmental process described by Piaget is of only a
narrow strand within the complex thread of human cognitive development. He focuses particularly for school-age children on a set of
logico-mathematical capacities which are no doubt important in
thinking, but hardly constitute its sum. To adopt a limited set of
psychological capacities as an end, a *telos*, for an educational program seems an unnecessarily harsh self-denying ordinance. Also, if
our *telos* in education is a kind of person, a description of, for example, Piaget's contentless formal operations cannot take us far in specifying our educational ideal.

Most people would, of course, see this kind of attempt to derive
educational goals from Piaget's theory as excessive. But the looking
for implications for educational practice, and for educational theories, in psychological theories is not at all uncommon.

One function of a theory is to focus our attention on a particular range of phenomena. The danger for educators in letting Piaget's theory focus our attention on the developmental process is that it will focus attention on phenomena of prime interest to the cognitive psychologist but of possibly only peripheral interest to the educator, and it will focus attention away from the phenomena of most direct interest and value to the educator. If we might expect to see quite different things when focusing on different aspects of the cognitive developmental strand, we might expect the strand of educational development to have even more distinct characteristics, highlights, stage divisions, and so on.

This directing—or misdirecting—of educators' focus onto phenomena that are of central interest to the developmental psychologist involves a number of, occasionally quite subtle, educationally destructive tendencies. It leads to the tendency to substitute intellectual development for educational development; to restrict attention disproportionately to logico-mathematical concepts at the expense of a variety of other mental furniture; to restrict educational goals to a kind of thinking rather than an image of a person; to introduce psychologically useful but educationally destructive distinctions, such as content/process, focusing attention on the latter and viewing the former as of merely instrumental value; to suggest inappropriate restrictions on what can be taught at any age, and how things can be taught; to suggest inappropriate criteria for recognizing and evaluating educational theories; and it leads to a number of other effects that follow from distortions of focus in the instrument we use to look at our phenomena of interest — that instrument being our theory.

The differences in what we might describe in the course of articulating an educational theory will be made clear in chapter five. The sketch of an educational theory given there will also demonstrate a curiosity about the end product of the process described and accounted for by an educational theory. It has been noted that education is not a "means-end" process, wherein things are done solely in order that they achieve a valued end. Rather each activity has to be justifiable on grounds of its own value. So the end product in education is constituted of the accumulation of activities that have formed the process. Piaget's theories, and some stage theories derived from them, have been called hierarchical-integrative theories. That is, the later stages incorporate the achievements or capacities of the earlier ones and extend them in new ways. Education seems to share this feature, and so educational theories should reflect it, but also education seems to be different in a significant way. Each stage of learning in education, indeed, leads to the development of capacities that are then integrated with more sophisticated capacities during the educational process. But in education each stage of learning also seems to lead to the development of capacities that are not so much integrated with more sophisticated capacities but rather that persist as more or less independent constituents that may flexibly be used in certain contexts and not in others. For example, as will be suggested in more detail in chapter five, during early adolescence children's learning seems especially sensitive to absorbing the romantic extremes of human experience (*Guinness Book of World Records* + heroes/ heroines + sentiment + action — in story form). One may see this period as that during which students learn to form powerful romantic associations with people, ideas, events, and so on. This capacity certainly may be developed and integrated with more sophisticated forms of understanding. But it also persists as something that becomes a more or less independent constituent of the later educated person. However advanced one's education becomes, he or she does not, or should not, lose the ability to form romantic associations with ideas, people, events, and so on. This doesn't mean that these associations should later be as uncontrolled as during early adolescence, but rather that this capacity does not become something quite different in the process of education. As a constituent capacity of an educated person, it remains as a source of vivifying knowledge, of imaginatively inhabiting the human experience that lies within written records of past events.

Thus, as our educational end product will be constituted of a set of such capacities, our educational theory will be describing its ideal end product as it describes the cumulative educational developmental process. This might also give us clues about the terms in which we can articulate our educational theory and our image of our ideal end product. If we cannot specify any knowedge, skills, and attitudes that are necessary in order to be considered educated, we can specify a set of necessary capacities. That is, if someone lacks the capacity to make, say, romantic associations with people, ideas, events, and so on, we might well conclude that a necessary ingredient of education is missing. (In chapter five a set of such necessary ingredients will be described.) It would seem, then, that one significant difference between a socializing theory and an educational theory is that the end product of the former will be articulated in terms of knowledge, skills, and attitudes, and of the latter will be articulated in terms of more diffuse capacities. If, for example, we were to describe what history adequate social agents should know, we could specify fairly easily that the main events leading to the formation of the society and culture around them should form the basis of their historical knowledge. If we were to describe what history adequately educated people should know, we could not similarly specify necessary content. Little knowledge about their own society's background and enormously detailed and sophisticated knowledge about some exotic time and place might well be an eccentric but adequate profile of an educated person. One could specify the educational requirement in terms of a capacity, which we might call historical consciousness. This capacity does not lend itself to precise specification, but this does not mean it is not a precise capacity. It means that it is complex and varied and may take different forms in each educated individual. It is perhaps simplistic to sum up by saying that socialization makes people more alike and education makes them more distinct. But the residue of truth in this simplification indicates why the end product to be described by a socializing and an educational theory will be quite different.

CULTURE-BOUND EDUCATION

The goal of education is not a kind of thinking or a body of knowledge, but rather a kind of person. It is a kind of person who will be in part composed of knowledge and thinking skills, along with a commitment to continue developing both. The process of psychological development may lead to certain thinking skills, like Piaget's formal operations, which may serve in a relatively innocent way as a terminus to the process. In education, however, the goal is a kind of person with certain characteristics, and this product serves as a justification for the process. We want to know what kind of person will be produced if we teach particular things, in particular ways, at particular times. A theory that outlines in detail the methods of teaching, the concepts, skills, and knowledge that will best lead toward the production of a Spartan warrior may be of little use to a typical small-town elementary school teacher. So the explicit specification of the goal is a necessary part of an educational theory.

It seems to follow that an education theory must be culture-bound in a manner against which psychological theories try to defend themselves. We will not seek to follow psychology's efforts to reduce the value-laden aspects of its theories. A value-free educational theory would be useless. We want to know how to produce a preferred kind of person; that is, we want to know what value decisions we should make at every step of the way. We want to know *what* we should teach in order to produce a person capable of enjoying and improving Western democratic social life and its culture (or some alternative), *how* we should teach those things to encourage the development of such a person, and *when* it is best to teach those things in those ways. The design of a curriculum to produce a particular kind of person requires answering these quetions, and it is a value-saturated and culture-bound task.

So an element of an educational theory will be a characterization of the desired end product of the educational process. In describing the desired end product, the theory must take into account the fact that humans are social and political as well as intellectual animals; that to specifiy a desirable educated person is to specify, implicitly or explicitly, a desirable political, social, and cultural context within which a particular set of desirable potentials are actualized.

A socializing theory is society-bound in that it is constrained to describe how to produce agents who will be effective within a particular society. It has no part then in recommending transformations of society, as it has nothing beyond present social utility to which it can refer. An educational theory may well prescribe an educational process whose products would transform present society, because it can refer to a cultural tradition of philosophical thinking about society. But that tradition is also a constraint on what the educational theory can prescribe. It can aim to transcend what that tradition has created, but such transcendence can only be achieved, can only be meaningful, if students are first initiated into that tradition. Freedom from its constraints, as it were, come only by passing through it, not be sidestepping it.

THE EMPIRICAL BASIS OF EDUCATIONAL THEORY

An educational theory may prescribe a process that no one has yet gone through. Indeed, the characterization of new ideals and of practical steps toward achieving them is a prime aim of the educational enterprise. If no one has yet gone through the process prescribed by the theory, it makes the question "What is its empirical basis?" rather complicated to answer. Such a question may initially mean: "Is there evidence suggesting that what the theory recommends involves things that are impossible?"

A "theory" offered in psychology without a substantial empirical base would be considered mere speculation. Should we, then, talk of educational speculations, rather than educational theories? We might note first that informed speculation, even in the natural sciences, may perform an important programmatic function. And it is not entirely irrelevant to add that in education the program is the point. Also, of course, the line between theory and speculation is not so clear as the words' usual positive and negative associations suggest.

The minimal requirements so far suggested for an educational theory are that it provide characterization of its ideal product and that this product be a recognizable kind of person, and that it tell us what things we should teach, how and when, in order to produce a person of this kind. So our educational theory will make at least one empirical claim: if you teach these things in this order in these ways then you will produce a person with these characteristics.

How can we test such a claim? We might try the program and see what happens. This is not, of course, altogether satisfactory. Given the human diversity apparent to casual observation, it may be that the ideal is accessible to only a small proportion of people and many people can be expected to achieve only some fraction of the ideal set of characteristics. Apart from specifying an ideal, then, we may expect our educational theory to specify educational goals that may be gained by people who have diverse capacities but who will not fully achieve the ideal. How does such a reasonable expectation affect our ability to test the single empirical claim we want our educational theory to make? Given the complexity of human beings, and the degree of individual variety, we may expect the general empirical test of the theory, which would involve implementing the program, to provide inconclusive results.

We may expect an educational theory to make many smaller-scale empirical claims. Testing these may either add to or reduce our sense of the plausibility of the theory's major empirical claim, but such smaller tests will rarely be adequate to undermine the general claim. Indeed an educational theory may systematically eradicate smaller-scale empirical claims, and propose a program whose justification at every step is tied to the end product. For example, if the theory claims that young people should learn by active discovery methods, empirical tests that show this to be a very inefficient method compared with what happens when traditional instruction is used need have no effect on the theory's plausibility. Its proponents may say that learning by active discovery is not recommended on the grounds of efficiency in mastering quantities of content, but is justified in terms of the character of the end product that will result if such methods are used.

A theory making only one empirical claim of such generality that its falsification is enormously difficult is still, of course, open to conceptual tests—of consistency, coherence, plausibility, and so on. Such conceptual testing, we may expect, will provide the major means for deciding which theory's programs are worthwhile implementing. The point, however, is that such a theory, if we desire its promised end product and think it offers a plausible way of bringing it about, is educationally useful. Indeed, such a theory tells us exactly the kinds of things we need to know in education. The character of theories in physics, psychology, and education may reasonably reflect the different functions they perform in these different areas and reflect differences in the phenomena they tell us something about. Educational theories may involve a greater degree of speculation than one would expect in psychology and they may not explain anything—unless one wants to speak loosely about explaining how to produce a particular kind of person. We may accept that they need to be formally falsifiable—we would want to rule out tautologous programs, which claim success if a particular procedure is followed regardless of its results — but we may acknowledge that empirically falsifying the most general claim of such a theory may be practically impossible.

An educational theory, then, must make at least one formally falsifiable empirical claim; it must distinguish the product of its program from the process—making the latter causally responsible for the former and making the former justify the latter.

We might, on the other hand, expect a socializing theory to yield much more readily to empirical testing. We will not expect it to prescribe a process no one has yet gone through. Rather we will expect it to describe a process that has to be gone through in order to accumulate the knowledge, skills, and attitudes required. As these can be fairly clearly specified, we can test empirically which method is best at inculcating them, and test which process produces the most adequate social agents. (That similar procedures of testing are inappropriate even for detailed parts of the educational program will be argued in more detail in chapter eight.)

CONCLUSION

The aim of this chapter has been to establish that there are properly some important differences between educational and socializing theories. The model that currently seems to dominate educational thinking and research is, we have suggested, a model proper to socializing theories. The influence of this discrimination is to displace educational activities and the acquisition of educational capacities — as distinct from socializing skills — from their proper place within what are called educational institutions.

For education to regain its proper role in schools, it seems to us necessary to become much clearer about distinctions between socializing and education, and so between socializing theories and educational theories. We need then to articulate educational theories that can serve the practical task of guiding what should be taught, when, and how, and in providing an image of an ideal educational product.[3]

CHAPTER FOUR

Varieties of Socialization

ALL CIVILIZATIONS have at some point asked what the purpose of (an) education ought to be. The very idea of civilization rests on the question and its answer. How should people change themselves through learning? What is most worth learning? Can this be taught to large numbers? Should any learning be required of everyone? Why? What would happen if this education is *not* undertaken successfully? How, and by whom, should education be provided, controlled, paid for?

In this chapter, we give a brief summary of the main approaches that have been taken toward an answer to this fundamental question, and then describe at greater length a contemporary approach that shows how education has become thoroughly confused with socialization. Through this detailed and critical description we show how much "educational" theory is not about education at all.

FIVE APPROACHES TO THE PURPOSE OF EDUCATION

The first is related to the idea of delight, especially the delight of mind that comes with apprehension of great things. This view claims that the best and most desirable of all values is found in intellectual pleasures—pleasures of the mind. Education's purpose, then, would be to expose individuals to that which gives such delight, and therefore to that which enriches one's well being. A.N. Whitehead's idea for the purpose of education was "exposure to greatness,"[1] and Matthew Arnold's was similar—"getting to know, on all the matters that most concern us, the best which has been thought and said in the world."[2] It is assumed in this view that greatness and excellence will produce a pleasurable state of mind in those who perceive them. In learning to delight in greatness and excellence, one learns to delight in learning itself, and one comes to believe Aristotle's suggestion that the greatest happiness is to be found in contemplation.

The second answer is a bit more worldly but still focused on the extraordinary. It suggests that education's purpose is to ensure good conscience in those whose actions will affect the social welfare. The politics of human affairs must be guided by persons of responsibility whose decisions are made wisely and are motivated by a firm moral integrity. One thinks of Thomas More in connection with this view of education as a precious and somewhat rare commodity.

The third approach is aimed at achieving an extension of culture through teaching individuals how to share in the tradition of values that forms the basis of their social institutions. This way of thinking about education puts great emphasis on preserving principles of conduct and on developing a sense of historical community in all the individuals of each new generation. Such an approach is sometimes closely tied to religious beliefs, but it need not be.

A fourth answer has been to devise ways of helping people to earn a living and to make sure that their lives were worth the living once they had sufficient means. It is the interest in the quality of one's existence that saves this approach from being merely another avenue to self-preservation through socialization. The problem has been that this interest in the quality of human experience has lost ground to the more directly job-related activities of schooling and has become relegated to a position of elective (that is, unnecessary) "enrichment."

Finally the most abstract and comprehensive approach to the purpose of education is the ironic one. The development of irony in one's perspective on life—including one's own education—is taken to be the ultimate triumph over innocence and its parochial constraints. Education in the ironic view provides an ability to appreciate and to discover new forms of complexity in all that one does and sees. It acts as protection against narrow-mindedness and oversimple, overconfident conclusions on those questions that matter very much in human affairs—such as, what the purpose of education is.

We turn now to a very different approach that stands in stark contrast to these five.

MUST WE EDUCATE?

This section takes its title from a book written by Carl Bereiter[3] on the question we have been discussing. We examine the way he deals with the issue of what education is because we think his book provides a good example of a contemporary frame of mind. It is a frame of mind that we do not share, and we think it rests on some serious and common faults in thinking about education. These faults are shared in large degree by the "back-to-basics" and the "minimum-competence" testing programs that have sprung up in the recent past. We focus on Bereiter's book to make our criticism of this frame of mind more explicit, but the criticism applies to many other works as well.

Bereiter is explicitly hostile to the very idea of educating in any of the five ways we have described, on grounds that public schools have no business teaching values, traditions, ironic points of view, or anything else that is meant to improve character or society or add to the quality of one's life.

Bereiter's is a book about educational theory that is at times both descriptive and prescriptive, but always normative. He attempts to do what one school of educational theorists and political statesmen have done in the past, namely, to articulate norms that either exist in present practice or are anticipated to exist imminently, in education per se or at least in the cultural milieux that support educational practices and institutions.

The role of a theorist who has taken on such a task as this is not so much to invent as to clarify, to impress us not so much with novelty as with acuity and sensitivity in examining crucial issues. Skill in doing this comes rarely because it is a refined skill that must be informed by considerable depth of study and by an appreciation for indispensable rules of analytic discourse.

We would like to consider Bereiter's book not only for its theoretical substance, but also, and more generally, as an example of a phenomenon of educational literature. This phenomenon is the publication of irriguous argument on subjects of theoretical and philosophical importance, written in such a way as to do for educational studies what the sober saga of a saucy seagull does for metaphysics.

The book is presented in two parts: "The Moral Dilemma of Education" and "Alternatives to Education." The author has his own doubts about the second part and solicits us to put it in its proper perspective; that is, "as a demonstration that alternatives do exist, and not as the presentation of a program which, if found wanting, can be picked apart and used as a sufficient reason to ignore the issues raised in the first part of the book. There are always alternatives to alternatives, and if the issues are valid they are worth considering in their own right."[4] We are respecting the wishes of the author and the credulity of the reader by considering the issues of the first part only, in their own right. It is fair, too, we think, to accept Bereiter's caveat that the book "is not a call to arms, but a call to the armchair."[5] He wishes to think deeply and theoretically about the moral "dilemma" of education, by which we understand him to mean the question of whether to educate at all.[6]

Bereiter's conclusions, his theoretical position on the "dilemma" he discusses, may be summarized briefly:

> Underlying my whole position on education is the belief that individual freedom should be maximized. I am opposed to public education because I see it as invading the most central area of individual freedom, the freedom to be the kind of person one is. . . .
>
> I would hold that the public employee — be he lawmaker, administrator, or teacher—who uses his position to educate, who performs his job with the ulterior motive of improving people and getting them to behave according to different values, is abusing his power. . . .
>
> Mass education is unavoidably authoritarian — a shaping of people according to the aims of those in power. . . .
>
> . . . the only kind of teaching that is truly nonauthoritarian is skill training, for competence in general gives the individual more power and freedom of choice. . . .
>
> It seems clear from the standpoint of human rights that public education is an anachronism. . . . Public education is grossly out of keeping with modern conceptions of freedom.[7]

Before examining these claims, and rather odd claims at that, considering they come from one who we had suspected was an educator by choice and by practice, we need to understand what Bereiter has in mind when he speaks of "education."

He gives us a definition early in the book: "To educate a child is to act with the purpose of influencing the child's development as a whole person."[8] He elaborates on this definition by implication in claiming that the role of a public school teacher is "the role of 'molder of citizens,' and 'shaper of the next generation'—a role that has been glorified in all the inspirational literature of education and taken for granted in educational philosophy and policy-making."[9] We have no idea what Bereiter reads for his inspiration, but it couldn't be educational philosophy. The list of philosophical works on teaching, the roles of teachers, and the development of character through education, which by no means "take for granted" Bereiter's own parochial view, is really too long to be included here, but it is easily long enough to show that such a claim as Bereiter would have us believe is utterly without defense.[10]

His definition itself is another matter. As we have learned from elementary texts in philosophical thinking,[11] one has some considerable berth in making different kinds of definitions. The one Bereiter gives is not the descriptive or reportive kind, for it does not show us how the term *education* has been used in common talk or in earlier times (we have dictionaries for this type of definition). His is rather a stipulative and programmatic definition, for he wishes to use the term in a certain (stipulated) and somewhat unusual way, from which follow strong behavioral (programmatic) implications; that is, in order to qualify as an "educator" one must "act with the purpose of influencing a child's development as a whole person," and if one does *not* so act, one must be doing something other than "educating."[12] Definitions of this word need not be evaluated for their approximations to truth or elegance; they need only serve to enlighten discourse between reasonable persons, especially when there are problems to be solved by the application of reason. The problem Bereiter is concerned with in his book is whether we must "educate," that is, whether anyone who teaches in a public school must or may or should act with the intention of influencing the development of a child as a whole person.

Does his definition serve to enlighten discourse on this problem? One way to test the question is to see whether it is *possible* to escape the programmatic or the stipulated aspects of the definition. Is it possible, for instance, to be a teacher (or even a trainer) without *intending to influence* the development of the child in some way? It is difficult to imagine a view of teaching or training that would allow such an unlikely possibility. It seems implicit in the notion of teaching and of training that some intent, with regard to student or trainee in relation to some subject or skill, is a necessary characteristic of the activity. Further, given the varieties of influence that are not only possible but likely to occur in human transactions, and with special attention to the inadvertent influence of social contexts themselves, one is pressed even to fabricate an example of "no influence" between persons in a relation of teacher-student or trainer-trainee.

Well, what about the other part of the definition, namely, the concept of a "whole person"? Bereiter is vague in using this term, but he apparently means the areas of attitudes and beliefs, the development of personality, values, intellect, and future role as an adult. Our challenge then, in determining a limiting condition to the definition is to discover some way to influence a child intentionally, without thereby influencing that child's personality, values, intellect, or future role as an adult, that is, some aspect of the whole person who is the child. Bereiter humbles us on this challenge; we are simply not up to it. Even if we agree with Bereiter that skill training[13] might be the answer, we have to confess in the next breath that learning a skill (e.g., reading, logic, or singing) might well alter one's "personality," if by that we mean all relevant aspects of a person that serve in some way to characterize one's appearance (to self and others), aptitudes, dispositions, regularities, and uniqueness. It might also influence one's values insofar as the skill may be perceived and felt to be important, since a held value *is* a perceived and felt importance; it might well influence intellect, too, if the skill happens to be reading or calculating; and if the skill is to be *used* at all, it cannot help but influence a future role as an adult. Perhaps if one were to teach a skill, as accidently and nonchalantly as possible (so as to minimize influence), and ensure that the skill would be useless and unappealing enough to be forgotten quickly (so as not to alter for very long any aspect of the person to whom the teaching was addressed) *then* one could truly avoid being an educator.

The problem, of course, is that one would not now be a "skill trainer" either, and the discourse that the definition was supposed to enlighten would be absurd. Whatever usefulness there might be in Bereiter's definition of education (for his argument in favor of skill training, at least) depends on its difference from skill training in terms of potential influence on some aspect of whole persons. As we have seen, for certain basic (reading), aesthetic (singing), and pragmatic (calculating) skill training, this is a distinction without a difference. Nevertheless, Bereiter makes much of this presumed difference, seeing "educating" as villainous and value laden, and supposing "skill training" to be virtually denuded of all moral character and implication for influencing the "whole person."

Some of Bereiter's convictions about education are shared, unlikely as it may seem, by Carl Rogers. Bereiter's underlying belief that "individual freedom should be maximized [as] the freedom to *be* the kind of person one is"[14] echoes Rogers' earlier declaration on the principle that one is entitled to the freedom in learning that is "the realization that 'I can live myself here and now, by my own choice.'"[15] Both base this conviction on a reverence for what each calls the "whole person," in recognizing the enormous importance of interplay between the more affective aspects and the more cognitive aspects of character, which we know is influenced by the interplay of environment and by more personal, indigenous forces. This conception of the importance of the "whole person" leads each to denounce teaching as an abuse of power but while Bereiter would prefer to become a "skill trainer' because he sees this as "the only kind of teaching that is truly nonauthoritarian,"[16] Rogers chooses instead to be a "facilitator" because "the only learning which significantly influences behavior is self-discovered, self-appropriated learning," and this of course cannot be taught, cannot be "directly communicated to another."[17]

The interesting thing about this comparison is that the same recognition of the concept of "whole person" and the same insight into the potential influence an adult could have on the development of one's freedom in being that "whole person" have led each to opposite pedagogical positions. Bereiter says because this influence is so important, teachers have no business paying any attention to it; they should confine themselves to skill training only, and let the parents decide what to do about their own child's "person." Rogers, however, argues that because this influence is so important, teachers ought to pay attention to "whole persons" *primarily*, and let the skills develop as a consequence of genuine interest and need as they arise. A healthy, strong self-concept, he claims, will lead naturally to the appropriate learning of skills, but skills without integrity as a person are beside the point, and dangerously disintegrating, fragmenting, of potentially whole persons.

This polarity has the suggestion of a genuine but not new dilemma in the history of educational thought, and not one without hope of resolution, either. We rely on Israel Scheffler's essay "Philosophical Models of Teaching" in showing how Bereiter is repeating worn controversy instead of raising promising new issues. Scheffler discusses three models of teaching that fundamentally describe our culture's basic orientations to teaching—each allowing for many variations, of course. The first, the *impression* model, whose empiricist variant is normally associated with Locke, he describes as "picturing the mind essentially as sifting and storing the external impressions to which it is receptive. The desired end result of teaching is an accumulation in the learner of basic elements fed in from without, organized and processed in standard ways, but, in any event, not generated by the learner himself."[18] This sounds very much like what Bereiter is *afraid* will happen if public school teachers are allowed to "educate" children, and very much like what he *assumes* will happen in "skill training." Bereiter errs in the traditional way by not recognizing two fatal difficulties in this thinking. First, the conception of the growth of knowledge in this model is false because it does not take into account, as Scheffler writes, that knowledge is "embodied in language, and involves a conceptual apparatus not derivable from the sensory data but imposed upon them. Nor is such apparatus built into the human mind; it is, at least in good part a product of guesswork and invention, borne along by culture and by custom."[19] And second, the impression model "fails to make adequate room for radical *innovation* by the learner."[20]

These two criticisms go to the heart of Bereiter's mistakes: he is at once afraid of a power that teachers simply do not have in the shaping of knowledge and values, and he assumes, falsely, that teaching by the name of "skill training" is somehow free of the same culture and custom, language and conceptual apparatus that both influence and limit the nature of "educating."

The second model Scheffler describes is the *insight* model. This view is at odds with the *impression* model in denying the possibility of conveying bits of knowledge into the student's mental account. "Knowledge, it insists, is a matter of vision, and vision cannot be dissected into elementary sensory or verbal units that can be conveyed from one person to another."[21] Scheffler refers us to St. Augustine's dialogue, "The Teacher," for a near perfect example of this model. St. Augustine argues that teachers convey knowledge by language, but language is mere noise unless the listener associates the language with an existing reality in his mind. Hence, a paradox: a teacher cannot teach new knowledge because the student will not understand what the teacher is saying unless the student already knows the realities to which the teacher refers. And if the student does not *already* know what the teacher means, the language will be mere noises. From this St. Augustine concludes that it is the teacher's role to prompt the student to seek realities not known to him already. "Finding these realities, which are illuminated for him by internal vision, he acquires new knowledge for himself, though indirectly as a result of the teacher's prompting activity."[22] Notice the remarkable similarity between being an Augustinian "prompter" and a Rogerian "facilitator" — both assume that really important knowledge cannot be directly communicated to another, but one can prompt or facilitate a search for it. This model makes some sense, if we allow that one can directly communicate new *information* at least, if not knowledge. Turning new *information* into knowledge is surely done by the knower primarily, with or without the help of a teacher's words. And it is just here that the insight model falters, as Scheffler suggests, by failing to account for "the processes of deliberation, argument, judgment, appraisal of reasons *pro* and *con*, weighing of evidence, appeal to principles and decision-making, none of which fits at all well with the insight model."[23] The other major fault with the model is its failure to admit that its teaching is oriented toward the development of character, as is all teaching, and that character goes beyond insight, just as it goes beyond impression. It involves judgments and principles of conduct that are related to, but more than, activities of cognition.

Scheffler's third model, one that we think would serve Bereiter well in understanding his own difficulties with conceptions of teaching, is called the *rule* model, and is associated with Kant. "For Kant . . . reason is a kind of justice to the evidence, a fair treatment of the merits of the case, in the interests of truth. In the moral realm, reason is action on principle, action that therefore does not bend with the wind, nor lean to the side of advantage or power out of weakness or self-interest."[24] From this it follows that teaching, or educating, even in Bereiter's weak definition of it, has the burden of developing character in the broadest sense of that term, "that is, principled thought and action, in which the dignity of man is manifest."[25] In this model, one can avoid the errors of the other two models, one can go beyond the highly questionable suggestion that adults have no business trying to influence a student's judgments and judgment-making abilities (as if they could *avoid* doing so), and one can also find room to say that the *autonomy of the student's judgment*, which is as well and fairly informed as possible, is the intended and highest value of teaching.

Such a conclusion resolves the dilemma set out at the beginning of this section and shows further that the dilemma is not a new one. It should be said, too, that the rule model is not free of weaknesses of its own. It is, for example, dependent on a certain tradition in reasoning, and like every tradition this one is not exempt from conceptual constraint and bias. However, assuming that one is taught to question even the "general principles to which one has bound oneself,"[26] and as long as one is taught to be vigilant in distinguishing reasons for accepting an idea from the ideas themselves as they compete for acceptance, then it seems the rule model is about as free of conceptual constraint as a model of teaching can be. In another sense, the model is weak for its missing concern with its own tradition, or with any tradition, and in this sense the model falters as a guide for coping with the powerful influences of the past in our present, which may or may not be "rational" or "reasonable." It is, nevertheless, of some credit to the model when we realize that it provides us the means for keeping distinct these influences as ideas and as reasons for accepting ideas.

There is a sense in which educational theories are social theories, and social theories are in the end moral conceptions. There is a sense, then, in which educational theories are moral theories.[27] This be-

VARIETIES OF SOCIALIZATION 53

comes clear as soon as one asks what education is *for,* as every educational theory must do. The answer will without fail articulate a way of life, or a preferred society, or an individual state of being that is logically connected to some moral reason or value. These moral reasons and values are in the end categorical, requiring no further appeal, though there may well be a series of intermediary reasons and values that are empirical and therefore subject to various tests and conditions of validity (these often will be the *technical* issues in the theory). But we always justify education in terms of how it is necessary (or at least germane) in preparing individuals for something, which is seen to be a *good* something, a norm or set of norms. The ultimate justification for education is the approximation or achievement of a norm or set of norms, in a social milieu. Such an activity is a moral one insofar as a norm is understood to require standards and principles that have to do with what *ought* to be done, and is not taken to mean, in the statistical sense, only what is or has been the case in a specified circumstance.

In the same way, if a particular type of skill training can be shown to have for its ultimate justification a moral value or reason, one can infer reasonably that the skill training will count in a fundamental way as education (though, of course, we are not obliged to say that *all* skill training regardless of its justification *must* be educational). In other words, one can determine whether skill training is a form of education by asking why the training is being undertaken, or is required. If we ask this question of Bereiter, the answer comes quickly: "Skill training can be justified on grounds that in the long run competence serves to liberate the learner from his teachers, as well as from others who have power over him, and it increases the options available to him, thus increasing his freedom."[28] Notice that skill training of the kind Bereiter has in mind can be justified on the grounds of the necessity of competence in gaining liberation from persons of power, and in generating options that lead to freedom. This is clearly a moral justification for skill training: one (the state?) has the right to impose or require skill training because it will prepare the individual for a preferred way of life or way of being that is characterized by competence, having options, and freedom from certain persons of power. Presumably Bereiter's vision includes the probability that many such persons together will bring about, or constitute, a "good" society. It sounds very much as if Bereiter has got himself a theory of "education" and not just "skill training," as he might prefer us to believe, although we would consider this educational theory incomplete. See chapter five for our reasons.

To be clear about what education we want, we must be clear

about what social values, what moral conditions we want. To do the former without first doing the latter is to perpetuate muzzy educational theory, or, as in Bereiter's case, to confuse theory with program and method.

In most versions of the democratic ideal, the underlying moral purpose is to perfect judgment and control the will, and to see that judgment is not usurped by the few on issues of major social importance for the many. In his monograph *Democracy, Stoicism and Education*, Robert Sherman indicates the long history of this view in discussing Epictetus' *Discourses:*

> The principal task of education is to perfect the judgment and reform the will. "Only show them their error and you will see how quickly they will desist from their mistakes" (Disc. i. 10. 3–4). How this perfection can be accomplished is outlined as the Stoic methodology; it is their epistemology. To perfect judgment and control the will, one must understand physical and logical matters. Physical study provides a knowledge of the facts of existence, and logical study is necessary to organize those facts and deduce from them correct judgments and appropriate courses of action.
> An understanding of logic is basic to morality.[29]

And, we might add, an understanding of logic is basic to educating, which itself is a form of morality.

The modern democratic ideal of freedom surrenders the conception of education as a weapon of the rulers, though education may be so abused for periods, especially during and after social crises. The ideal holds instead that education must influence students, not by the insidious shaping of attitudes beneath a guise of objectivity or some sort of secular crusade, but by developing capacity and allegiance for reason and principled action. This kind of influence is not always successful, though, because being reasonable is an arduous, exacting achievement, and principled action requires commitment to a morality more demanding than ordinary self-interested gain seeking. This is quite different from being "unavoidably authoritarian" or out of keeping with any modern conception of freedom.

It is not as if we had a choice whether to educate; Bereiter's is an empty question. We live and justify the raising of children with social theories, which are moral theories, and part of each is an educational theory. Education, as preparation of individuals for some social or personal good, therefore, is inescapably a moral undertaking, even when someone calls it "skill training," if it is justified, as it must be, by appeal to normative reasons and values. That we cannot avoid these circumstances, however, does not mean that we are *subject* to them *as they are* at any given time. Although it seems that we cannot choose whether to educate, we can choose how to think and go about educating. Dashing back to defeasible conceptions of mind, knowledge, and the illusion of a value-free, asocial, amoral skill training as an alternative is hardly helpful. Such an argument, put forward as "new" or "challenging," is itself a reminder that to be an educator, one first needs to be educated.

Perhaps the best way to summarize the difficulties we have with the kind of thinking Bereiter's book represents is to quote him one last time on the subject of helping teachers find common ground, or harmony, with students. He says:

> One remedy is to educate teachers in moral and educational philosophy, to make them conscious and critical of the values they promote. But that is not an acceptable remedy in a free society. If all teachers were philosophers they might be wiser, but this still would not entitle them to determine what kind of people their students should develop into. A wise despot is still a despot.[30]

We haven't much left to say of the kind of thinking that does not distinguish between philosophy and despotism, and whose very claim to acquaintance with the former must now be held questionable. But we do have more to say on the subject of teaching moral and educational philosophy in chapter six.

CHAPTER FIVE

Toward an Educational Theory

IN 1959 David P. Ausubel noted that the scientific study of growth and development had made great advances but could still offer "only a limited number of very crude generalizations and highly tentative suggestions"[1] to the educational practitioner. Since 1959 there has been rapid growth in our knowledge of psychological, moral, social, physical, conceptual, and other kinds of development. Vast amounts of empirical research have probed and tested the various theories advanced, forcing further revisions and refinements, and the practical activities of teaching and learning. Today we may confidently claim that these disciplines still offer the educational practitioner only a limited number of very crude generalizations and highly tentative suggestions.

Why is this? It seems so intuitively obvious that a refined theory and its supporting knowledge about, say, concept development, should be directly applicable to education. Why do such theories yield only crude generalizations and vague recommendations of no greater precision that any teacher with half a grain of common sense can offer? Ausubel claimed it was due to the failure to appreciate the distinction between a pure and an applied science. The disciplines that study development, learning, and motivation aim to discover general laws as ends in themselves. Ausubel pointed out that application of the discoveries of the pure sciences to practical educational situations requires additional research "at the engineering level of operations." Furthermore, according to Ausubel, the intuitive sense that one can go directly from the findings of these pure sciences to education "has caused incalculable harm," and has led to "fallacious and dangerous . . . overgeneralized and unwarranted applications"[2] in educational theory and practice.

The claim that educational applications of theories generated in "pure" disciplines have been at best vacuous and at worst dangerous represents a powerful challenge to the major industry concerned with communicating these theories and their "implications" to teachers and education students. The challenge is made even stronger by the plausibility of the claim, especially if the typical text for an introductory psychology of education course is to count as evidence. There we find lengthy sections on, say, Piaget's theory of stages of development, with a brief concluding section labeled something like "Implications for Teaching," which announces that one should not use an exclusively verbal method of presentation to very young children or expect the young to understand very abstract concepts. These "insights" hardly come as news to the average teacher.

This is not at all to depreciate Piaget's work. Part of a proper appreciation of its value involves not abusing it by trying to extend it in ways that are facile and inappropriate. Piaget has contributed enormously to our understanding of children's intellectual development. The *focus* of his theory, however, is not education but genetic epistemology. The knowledge that generated the theory and the further knowledge and inquiries generated by the theory are determined by the theory's focus. The fact that teachers are interested in certain topics he has studied does not magically convert his theories and knowledge into a form directly applicable to education's practical concerns. At present it seems that educational research is dominated by psychological theories, which lead to knowledge of psychological value and interest, but which offer only occasional "implications" for education. An educational theory of learning, development, or motivation should be composed from, and focus back onto, those phenomena of greatest interest to educators, and such a theory will likely involve a different level of generality and a different range of phenomena than those that interest psychologists, sociologists, or genetic epistemologists.

Ausubel claims that before developmental theories can yield fruit for the typical teacher preparing a physics or social studies class, a further level of research needs to be carried out. Well, maybe. The research carried out so far at this "engineering level" does not encourage us to wait for more with bated breath. The theories this "engineering" research is to draw from are not educational theories either; they do not focus on the *complexity* of educational concerns. They encourage, indeed force, the "engineer" to share their narrow concern and specialized focus. Typically, such research lacks the precision and control of purer research, and has provided no greater insights for practice than the crude generalizations and tentative suggestions we have had by the cartload.

No: as we have argued in the previous chapters, what we need in education is a *different kind* of theory — one that focuses on the educational aspects of development, learning, and motivation: one that directly yields principles for engaging children in learning, for unit and lesson planning, and for curriculum organizing at each stage of a typical person's development.

These are, of course, somewhat opaque claims. In education we are so bemused by imported theories that the demand for a theory dealing with the phenomena of most interest to us leaves us wondering what such a theory would look like. The only relatively recent attempt to sketch an educational theory that conforms with the criteria laid out in chapter three is Whitehead's, though that is very much a bare-boned sketch.[3] What makes it an *educational* theory, however, is simply the fact that it deals with the level of phenomena of direct interest and use to educators.

What follows then is our version of much the same thing. This chapter is entitled "Toward an Educational Theory" because its primary purpose is not to offer a comprehensive and systematically worked-out theory, but rather to identify the kinds of phenomena from which an educational theory of development—or rather a theory of educational development—may be built, and to organize them into a rough general scheme. The focus will be on the main categories children seem to use at different ages to make best sense of the world and experience. If this scheme seems plausible, revision and refinement may follow, based on further observation and empirical testing.

This scheme distinguishes four main stages of educational development, the mythic, romantic, philosophic, and ironic. The following four sections describe the main characteristics of each stage and indicate roughly what seem to be the main characteristics of the processes of transition from one stage to the next. The concluding section discusses why these stages might be seen as taking us toward a theory of educational development. It is important to develop an image of an educational theory so as to begin (re)building defenses against the modern incursion of socialization and its agent, educational psychology.

THE MYTHIC STAGE

Where might we look for clues as to the main categories young children use in being able to make best sense of the world and experience? We might sensibly look to those things which engage them most powerfully and seem to be most clearly meaningful to them. Children's stories and games, then, might provide fruitful subjects to begin with. We are familiar with the fact that as children mature, they like different kinds of stories. Similarly, as Iona and Peter Opie have observed:

> When generalizing about children's play it is easy to forget that each child's attitude to each game, and his way of playing it, is constantly changing as he himself matures; his preferences moving from the fanciful to the ritualistic, from the ritualistic to the romantic (i.e., the free-ranging games, "Hide and Seek," "Cowboys and Indians"), and from the romantic to the severely competitive.[4]

It is worth noting also that young children's stories and games have important features in common. They both have beginnings, middles, and ends; they reduce and limit reality, providing an arena within which children may feel secure; the meaning of behavior is clearly and precisely established; they tend to share imaginative content built on binary opposites — fairies and witches, cops and robbers, war and team conflicts—that are in turn based on underlying, though controlled, concepts of good and bad, love and hate, fear and security, and so on.

For economy's sake, only stories will be considered in the following. The underlying characteristics that are exposed by analyzing those stories which most powerfully engage young children's interest may help expose important categories of their thinking.[5] Such stories lack realistic concepts of action, place, change, causality, and so on; they make little call on the simultaneous combination of ideas; the number of characters is small and homogeneous; the characters are composed from one or two outstanding characteristics (big and bad, beautiful and industrious, etc.); the characters are differentiated by simple contrasts or binary opposites (rich or poor, big or little, obedient or disobedient, clever or stupid, etc.); meaning is always clear, in the sense that it is always clear who is to be approved or disapproved of, and what one should feel about the events.

Such stories raise two questions that take us further toward underlying categories of young children's thinking: why do stories as such work so powerfully at engaging interest, and why is the particular and peculiar content of young children's stories so engaging — things like monsters and witches, and talking animals and trees?

Perhaps the most important feature of a story is that it is the linguistic unit that can ultimately fix the meaning of the events that compose it. Take, for example, the event, "He shot Tom." By itself the event is not very meaningful; we don't know how or why he shot Tom, or who he and Tom are, or, most important, whether to feel glad or sorry that he shot Tom. The only linguistic unit that can answer all these questions finally is the story. The story, as Aristotle pointed out, has a beginning that sets up expectations, a middle that complicates them, and an end that satisfies them. Within a story the meaning of events may be ultimately fixed—as it never can be in history and "real life." Each event has a place in the whole, and we know we have reached the end of a story when we know what to feel about all the events that compose it.[6]

That is to say, the story form is not simply a means of casual entertainment for young children, but it reflects fundamental categories of young children's thinking. It is important here, because the story is the linguistic unit that can fix meaning and feeling about its contents precisely, and we know from children's frequent demands for absolute explanations—even when they are quite inappropriate—that the need to know what to feel about something is important for them to be able to make sense of it. Because the story form is the only means we have of absolutely fixing the meaning of things in this effective sense, it seems reasonable that we should use it in organizing knowledge so that children might best learn.

This stage is called "mythic" because young children's thinking seems to share a number of important characteristics with the kind of thinking evident in the stories of myth-using people.[7] The strange monsters and humanized animals that inhabit children's stories seem similar to the creatures found liberally in myth stories, and a similar explanation for both seems reasonable. Myth stories tend to be articulated on binary opposites, as are those stories that appeal most powerfully to young children. In the case of myth stories, the oppositions may be between important elements in the life of their users: nature/culture, life/death, raw/cooked, honey/ashes. In the mental life of children, important basic oppositions include big/little, love/hate, security/fear, courage/cowardice, good/bad. Typical fairy stories are built on sets of such binary opposites. So children tend initially to make sense of things in binary terms, using only a couple of concepts at one time. These binary opposites are then elaborated by a process of mediation between the binary poles. For example, the concepts of "hot" and "cold" will normally be learned as the first temperature distinctions. These will then be mediated by "warm," or by "quite hot" and "quite cold." Thereafter children may learn to mediate between "cold" and "warm," and "warm" and "hot," leading gradually to a set of concepts along the temperature continuum. Attempts to mediate between other binary opposites perceived in their environments lead to more than simple conceptual elaborations along continua or size, speed, temperature, and so on. When the same process tries to mediate between humans and animals, we get those dressed and talking bears, dogs, and rabbits that play so prominent a part in children's imagination. Attempts to mediate between life and death give us ghosts and spirits of various kinds—things that are both alive and dead, as things warm are both hot and cold.

This is not to suggest that children at the mythic stage can understand things only if they are put in terms of binary opposites. Greater or lesser elaboration between binary opposites will have been achieved depending on the degree of progress they have made through the stage. The point is that binary opposites are still fundamental to children's thinking at this stage, in that even though considerable elaboration from the initial binary terms may have been achieved, meaning derives most clearly from the basic binary distinctions. That is, if something is to be most clearly meaningful, it should be built on, elaborated from, clear binary opposites.

Claude Lévi-Strauss' analyses of myth stories conclude that they too are built on, or elaborated from, basic binary opposites perceived in their user's environments. Lévi-Strauss has also argued, drawing on Roman Jakobson's work in phonetics,[8] that the kind of binary thinking alluded to is basic to all thought, and reflects a basic structure of the human mind. Whether or not this is the case, it is evident that such binary structures are prominent in young children's thinking.

In addition, myth stories and children lack what has been generally called a sense of "otherness": concepts of historical time, physical regularities, local relationships, causality, and geographical space. Some analysts of myth suggest one of the functions of myths is to "obliterate history," to assert that nothing has changed in the world since the sacred beginning, thus providing a kind of eternally valid "charter" for things as they are. Children's lack of the concepts of "otherness," however, may be accounted for simply as a lack of experience and knowledge of change and causality on an historical scale in a geographical arena.

A further, connected feature of mythic thinking is its lack of a clear sense of the world as autonomous and objective. The world is not conceived of as an impersonal, objective entity. Such a conception is that achievement of a mature rationality. The child's world is full of entities charged with, and given meaning by, those things the child knows best: love, hate, joy, fear, good, bad. Things are perceived as feeling, willing, and thinking like the child. The world is, as it were, absorbed into the child's vivid mental life. Much more than is the case for an adult, children's imaginative life colors and charges their environment with a meaning derived from within. Piaget has expressed this well in the observation that at this age there is "a sort of confusion between the inner and the outer, or a tendency to fix in objects something which is the result of the activity of the thinking subject."[9]

So, learning at this mythic stage seems to involve making sense of the unknown world "without" in terms of the known world "within." The things children have to learn will include those fundamental categories characterized above. These are the intellectual tools and conceptual categories they can employ in making sense of the outside world. The process of learning at the mythic stage, then, involves projecting these known things onto the outside world and as it were, absorbing the world to them. As these are the major categories by means of which young children derive meaning from the world, so they are the major categories according to which we must organize knowledge to be most meaningful to young children.

Initially, then, the world becomes known in terms of the basic forms and characteristics of children's mental life. It could hardly be otherwise. Learning is a matter of connecting the known categories to the "outside" world and fitting the things in the world to them. The clearer the connection between categories and things in the world, the more successful should be the learning. (As children develop through the mythic stage, knowledge about the world increasingly expands the initial set of categories. Not only does the world provide knowledge as such, but things in the world become, as it were, things the child thinks with. So concept and content feed each other by dialectical interaction.)

The characteristics sketched above seem to be prominent in children's thinking until about eight, nine, or ten. Sometimes during this period some significant changes occur, leading to the move from the mythic to what we call the romantic stage.

THE ROMANTIC STAGE

The move from the mythic to the romantic stage takes place roughly at age ten, and the new phase lasts until age fifteen or sixteen. The move may be seen in the development of rudimentary but serviceable concepts of "otherness"; concepts of historical time, geographical space, physical regularities, logical relationships, and causality. In developing through the mythic stage, children seem to perceive increasingly clearly that the fundamental emotional and moral concepts derived from a knowledge of self, family, and basic human relationships are inadequate to make full sense of the "outside" world that they are learning about. Knowledge and experience of the world provide the concepts of "otherness." It is in this sense that children begin to use the world to think with. Chairs and countries are increasingly clearly seen to be inadequately conceived of as thinking, willing, and feeling entities, and they begin to generate in the child concepts appropriate to their particular forms of being and behavior. Another way of putting this is to say that the passage from the mythic stage coincides with the perception that the world is autonomous, separate, and fundamentally different from the child.

Children, then, face two connected tasks in order to reestablish a sense of intellectual security in this newly perceived alien world: first, they must forge a new relationship and "connections" with the autonomous world and so achieve some method of dealing with its threatening alienness, and, second, they have to establish a sense of their distinct identity.

How do they achieve these? Again, we might look for clues in the content and form of the kinds of stories that most powerfully engage children at this romantic stage. A "romantic" story in this sense is one in which a hero or heroine (or institution, nation, idea, etc.), with whom or with which the reader may identify, struggles against odds to a glory and transcendence over threatening nature (or events, institutions, ideas, nations, etc.), in which glory the reader may then share. Such stories have a crucial characteristic that makes them ideal for this stage—they are ego-supporting. They allow, and encourage, the reader to associate with some noble and powerful force that achieves success against a threatening world. (Occasionally they allow the hero or heroine to die or lose, but only in a context which enables the reader deliciously to share the hero's or heroine's moral or other superiority, which is not recognized by the unfeeling world.)

K. Bühler calls the stories that most appeal at this stage the "Hans Christian Andersen-type."[10] They have more complex plots than those which appeal at the mythic stage. They are realistic. Even when they deal with imaginary worlds, there is always a concern with realistic details or plausibility. They have clear and powerful heroes and heroines. They tend to have exotic, though realistic or plausible, settings. They are often concerned with the differences between people, who have more complex motives than in the mythic stories.

Their meaning is always clear in the sense that readers know clearly what they should feel about the events and characters. Bühler mentions *Robinson Crusoe* as a paradigm of this kind of story.[11] One might add much of science fiction, adventure stories, and animal stories.

Given these as prominent characteristics of romantic stories, we may infer that students respond to the threat posed by the newly perceived alien world primarily by associating with those elements in the world that are most powerful, noble, courageous, in short, with those things that preeminently transcend the threats the world poses to the immature ego.

An association with the ingenuity and courage of Ulysses or Captain Kirk of the Starship *Enterprise,* or with the nobility and determination of Florence Nightingale, or St. Teresa of Avila involves the student's ego in the implicit claim that "I could do that too," or rather, "I *am* doing that too." Students, then, no longer need to fear the vast mysterious world that is opening up before them because they can transcend every threat by means of romantic associations. By such means the threats are transmuted into adventure.

This capacity to associate oneself with powerful forces, characters, movements, ideas seems to be a development of the mythic capacity to "connect" with the world by means of those best-known emotions and bases of morality. Just as the child at the mythic stage can absorb any information provided in these familiar terms, the student at the romantic stage may form associations with anything in the universe embodying those qualities which best transcend the challenges posed by daily living in the real world — qualities like courage, nobility, fortitude, genius, power, energy, and creativity.

The TV shows that are most popular with students at this stage seem to share these characteristics. The Bionic Woman and the Six Million Dollar Man exemplified the desire to transcend the world while remaining in it, to be, like a more persistent hero, both Clark Kent and Superman. The more adult the target audience for these romantic figures, the more subtle is the fusion of everyday and transcendent in the hero or heroine. These characters are, in our terms, romantic not mythic because of the attempt to relate them to the everyday world of reality. As with Superman's birth and escape from the dying planet Krypton, so the etiology of the Six Million Dollar Man and his bionic ladyfriend is important for suggesting that they inhabit a real or possible world. No attempt is made to suggest a plausible or possible world in which the mythic Korky the Cat or Biffo the Bear live, dressed in ordinary clothes, standing on two legs, in a fairly standard middle-class environment.

At the mythic stage, the mind's categories largely determined how the world was perceived to work. At the romantic stage, the student's mind has to accommodate itself to the alien rules of how the world in fact works. That is to say, students have to develop their romantic sense of identity within a context of *reality*. The typical romantic manner of exploring and discovering what is real and possible in the world seems to involve a development of the mythic thinker's use of binary opposites. Instead of projecting binary opposites from "within," however, the romantic mind searches outside itself to the *limits* of the world for external binary opposites within which reality exists.

A defining characteristic of the move into the romantic stage, then, is the development of a quite sudden fascination with the extremes of what exists and what is known. In the mythic stage, the sense of scale pays no heed to the limits imposed by reality; going toward the king's throne, the hero may have to pass a series of guards, the biggest of which is three miles high and the smallest of which is no larger than your thumbnail. At the romantic stage, students' interest in scale similarly focuses on the extremes, but is constrained by reality. Thus the *Guinness Book of World Records* fascinates the romantic student, with its accounts of the biggest, the smallest, the fastest, the highest, the farthest, and so on. It is between such extremes that students locate reality, and within them that they construct their identity.

This stage is called romantic because it shares with romanticism the tension that comes from the desire to transcend a threatening reality while seeking to secure one's identity within it. The mythic project that treated reality with contempt has now to be, reluctantly, confined within it. So romance is, as it were, myth confined to the real world, but constantly beating against its limits.

An important characteristic of knowledge that engages students at the romantic stage, then, is that it tells them something about what is real and possible. The impossible fantasies of the mythic stage are quite suddenly treated with contempt as "stupid kids' stuff." A further characteristic required for knowledge to be engaging at this stage is that it must be *different*, different from everything mundane and conventional, different from everything the students have known and experienced. Just as romantic exploration of the real world begins with the probing of its limits, so it is the fantastic and spectacular that the romantic perception highlights.

One reflection of students' desire to explore limits and to form personal associations with whatever is to be learned leads them to want to know "what it was like then, or there, or doing that." They want to sense different forms of human life, but not in the way that a typical scholar might. Their concern is to feel different forms of life, to try them on, as it were. Realistic detail, then, becomes important. The more different from the student's experience it is, the better. Incas and an imaginary Martian colony have a head start over the histories and lives of their grandparents. The association is made personal not through proximity of relationship or physical familiarity, but through those human qualities which lead to transcendence over the everyday and commonplace world. Grandparents' lives can, of course, be made engaging by these principles, but in general it seems much easier to engage typical teen-age students at a romantic stage with stories about a medieval scholar/saint like Ramon Lull than with knowledge about grandparents' lives. On the same grounds, then, it is not the development of the students' own society that will be most engaging, but that of the most exotic and bizarre societies. Having established a sense of the limits of possible societies, they will have a framework to begin making sense of their own. Before they develop such a framework, details of their society will be likely to remain largely meaningless in any educational sense.

A further characteristic of students' thinking at this stage is indicated in the frequently observed development of obsessive hobbies and pastimes. There is a desire to learn something exhaustively or collect something completely, to know the score of every football game played by the team with which an association is formed, to collect every postage stamp of a particular era and place, to know every detail of the life and collect every photograph of a film star or member of royalty, to know the shape of every leaf of every tree, to know everything about Saturn or about costumes through the ages. It is a kind of intense specialization, but we think it is more properly seen as a further expression of the desire to find the limits of things. By exhaustively knowing *something*, one gets a sense of the scale of everything.

THE PHILOSOPHIC STAGE

The focus of this characterization is on the stages of educational development of people who become in our sense "well educated." The outline is of something more near to an ideal than to a norm. This needs to be noted here because a very large proportion of our children in public schools seem to reach this philosophic stage only in the most tenuous way, if at all. The philosophic stage seems to coincide with the last years of high school and with the early undergraduate years.

At the romantic stage students' perceptions focused on the extremes, on the most fascinating bits and pieces, on vivid "true" stories, on dramatic events and ideas, on bizarre facts, on heroes and heroines, and on some particular areas in great detail. There was, of course, the realization that all these were parts of the same world, but the connections between the parts were not a matter of much concern. Students "connected" themselves with these elements directly by means of romantic associations. One aspect of the move from the romantic to the philosophic stage may be seen in the strengthening realization that all the bright bits and pieces are interconnected parts of some general unit. History, for example, is increasingly seen less as a set of stories, a set of styles of living, and more as a continuum of styles, a single complex story. This shift involves the students' realization that they are not as free as they had thought; they are entrammelled in the world as in a spider's web.

The relatively rapid decay of the romantic world view requires that students establish a new kind of intellectual security within this newly perceived world. To do this they have to establish their place and their roles in the natural, social, and historical *processes* of which they are becoming aware. From being transcendent players, they have to become *agents*.

The means whereby this new security is established seems to follow from students' perception of themselves as parts of complex processes. If they are parts of complex processes, then the way to understand their proper roles within them is to find out the truth about these processes. The major defining characteristic of the philosophic stage, then, is the search for the truth about human psychology, for the laws of historical development, for the truth about how societies function. That is, the philosophic focus is on the general laws whereby the world works. By knowing these, the students will know their proper places and roles, and so they will securely know themselves.

Whereas at the romantic stage students developed a sense of the limits of reality, a sense of its scope and scale, at the philosophic stage they turn inward, as it were, to conduct a general survey of the real world and begin to chart a mental map of its general features.

In the *Poetics*, Aristotle distinguishes between history on the one hand and poetry and fiction on the other, on the grounds that the former is concerned with establishing particular truths whereas the latter are concerned with more general or philosophic truths — a historian is concerned with whether this or that happened whereas a poet is concerned with what happens of necessity, with the general laws of things. It is on the basis of this distinction that this stage is called philosophic. The students' interests are little engaged by particular knowledge for its own sake; they are primarily engaged by the kinds of pursuits Aristotle thought proper to the poet, that is, finding general truths about natural, social, psychological or historical processes.

It seems that the endless particulars that students learned during the romantic stage, and that were made meaningful by romantic association, now threaten to be merely chaotic bits and pieces littering the mental landscape. To be made "philosophically" meaningful requires that the particulars be organized within some general scheme. The first move of this "mental map-making" stage seems to be to establish a sense of the main features and their relationships and locate the particulars within the general context.

To turn to the study of history for an example: at the philosophic stage a student might be attracted by a fairly simple form of Marxism because it offers a means of readily organizing a vast range of particulars. It provides an enormously general scheme through which *all* history, all the phenomena of the past (and present and future too), can be reduced from their unmanageable diversity to a relatively simple process. Once one understands the process, "the laws of history," then the details may be swept up, slotted into their places in the process, and so be made meaningful. All that knowledge learned at the romantic stage about knights and peasants and the great artists of the Renaissance suddenly is endowed with a new meaning as part of the decay of feudalism and the rise of the bourgeoisie. That is, the *meaning* of the particulars is now derived primarily from their place within the general scheme.

Such a scheme, which determines the meaning not only of the past but of the present and future as well, seems also to provide students with a means of understanding their proper roles as agents within the historical process. If they accept the simple Marxist view, for example, they know that their proper role in Western societies should involve them in exacerbating the contradictions of capitalism, hindering the plans of reactionary bourgeois forces, and furthering the cause of the proletariat. If they accept a liberal progressive view, their roles as agents will involve them in defending and strengthening the liberal institutions of their society.

So this "philosophic" craving for generality seems to be the means whereby chaotic particular knowledge about the world is reduced to manageable proportions. This urge toward the general leads students to develop the abstract intellectual tools necessary for imposing order on the most complex phenomena.

Thus, quite suddenly, very general concepts like "society," "culture," "the mind," "evolution," "human nature," and so on become prominent in students' language and thinking. The complex of social interactions, of institutions, of people and their jobs and families, of buildings and forms of transport, and a million and one other things are reduced to concepts like "society" or "culture," and may be juggled with a few equally general concepts to establish for the students enormously general principles about how the world works. From these they form ideologies and metaphysical schemes: intellectual tools with which they can organize, simplify, and reduce even the greatest complexities with casual confidence. Ideologies and metaphysical schemes represent the boldest lines that give order to the students' mental map of the world. They become the fixed co-ordinates by means of which all particulars and details are located and given meaning.

Another apparent reflection of this urge toward imposed order is the development of hierarchies. If one begins to appreciate music at this stage, the philosophic impulse is to ask who is the best composer and the second best, the third best, and so on. The impulse at this stage is toward discovering the most powerful criterion that will allow one to organize all composers (or football players, or actors, or automobiles, or whatever) by slotting them into place in a hierarchy. Frequently this leads to the imposition of single-criterion hierarchies where they are inappropriate, where multiple criteria should be applied.

The philosophic students' prime requirement, however, seems to be to get some kind of control over the bewildering, and threatening, diversity of the phenomena under consideration. The philosophic impulse is to establish a first general ordering on some useful criterion. The refinements and sophistications can only follow an initial general ordering.

This search for the criteria by which things may be ranked in hierarchies seems to be a development from, but is also different from, the romantic collecting and organizing of something in great detail. The focus of interest at the philosophic stage has moved from the particulars to the principles by which the particulars may be ordered. At the romantic stage, the particulars and their immediate relationships provide the focus of interest. The philosophic concern with recognizing the best composer, is not a romantic search for extremes, rather it is a part of the philosophic search for a criterion whereby all composers can be ranked.[12]

Once one has identified *the right* criterion for evaluating and ranking composers, or comedians, or novels, or football players, or once one has found the ideology that shows *the truth* about historical and social processes, one can feel confident in dealing with particular composers, novels, or historical facts and events; it becomes a simple job of slotting them into place. It is a characteristic of students at the philosophical stage to be confident or overconfident, that they know the meaning of everying. Indeed, the abusive observation often made about students at this stage is that "they think they know everything." This is precisely so. They *do* think they know the true meaning of everything, even of things they have not yet learned. That is, they think they understand the general principles from which the meaning of particulars is derived; thus knowing *the truth* in general, they see learning and organizing the particulars as essentially a trivial task.

Students at this stage often become impatient with learning further details, and become contemptuous of those scholars who seem interested in particulars for their own sake. Such scholars are dismissed as "fact-grubbers," as narrow-minded, and blind to the greater scheme of things.

A rough attempt to characterize the process of development through this stage leads to an image of a dialectical movement between accumulating knowledge and increasing sophistication of the general scheme or ideology. For example, if one accepts the simple Marxist ideology, then one's interest is focused by that ideology onto the particular knowledge that best clarifies and supports it. In the course of accumulating such knowledge, however, one will learn things that seem at first sight anomalous in light of the simple ideology. The typical response will be to make the ideology more sophisticated to accommodate this knowledge. To support the more sophisticated ideology one needs to accumulate further knowledge, some of which will be likely to be anomalous to the more sophisticated scheme, focusing further sophistication and revisions, and so on and on.

From this sketch of some important characteristics of students' thinking at this stage, it may seem the story form plays no significant role in their organizing of knowledge. But there does remain a significant feature of the story form. What we see in moving from the mythic, to romantic, to philosophic stage, is a reduction in the simplicity and determining force of the story form. And while the form is so weakened by the philosophic stage that we do not normally recognize it, exposing its persisting force seems important because of the implications that follow for how we should organize material so that it is best understood and used by students.

As shown above, the story form is different from reality in that the story ends; reality goes on, and we are in the very middle. An important feature of typical philosophic generalized schemes is that they create a unit out of disparate pieces; conceptualizing a process requires the imposition of some beginning and end. This may be seen most clearly with regard to history. In order to conceive of history as a single process one has to apply a kind of "plot" to it. Marxism, for example, sees history as a dialectical struggle of classes with conflicting interests that will finally be resolved in a classless society. That "finally" is important. Inherent in the description of the process is the assertion of how it will end. Similarly other philosophic ideologies imply how the process will eventually unfold.

The function of imposing an end, as discussed earlier, is to be able to impose determinate meaning on the elements that make up the process. By "knowing" that there will be a dictatorship by the proletariat, the Marxist "knows" the true meaning of the class conflict in the past and present. So the confidence (overconfidence) about knowing the true meaning of things is achieved by use of the central feature of the story form.

The kinds of stories that seem to appeal most at this stage may be described as the literature of ideas. A writer like Jorge Luis Borges appeals strongly to the philosophic intelligence. His brief stories that he calls "inquisitions" involve primarily a play with ideas and a relative absence of the simple story form and of exploring human motivations and character. Typically, philosophic literature is poor in its presentation of individual human variety. People tend to be typed and their role is to give movement to, or embody, ideas.

THE IRONIC STAGE

In the philosophic stage students focus on abstract general schemes as the sources of truth. Progress through the stage seems to be marked by an increasing sophistication of the schemes in response to accumulating knowledge. The transition from the philosophic to the ironic stage, then, seems to come with students' appreciation that no general scheme can adequately reflect the richness and complexity of reality. That is, the general schemes break down under the weight of anomalous particulars.

This stage is called "ironic" because its key characteristic seems to be a clear sense of what the mind contributes to knowledge. Put more gnomically, it represents a clear appreciation of where we end and the world begins. At each of the previous stages there is some confusion about this: things that are a product of our modes of perception or manner of organizing knowledge are assumed to be a part of the world. This is exemplified at a simple level by young children's assumption that the moon follows them along the street, or in a more complex way by the philosophic assumption that an ideology imposed on history is a part of historical reality. Or, more subtly yet, it is exemplified in our tendency to reify concepts and by the general bewitchment language spins around our perception and understanding.

St. Paul observed that when he was a child he thought in a childish way, but that on becoming a man he left the characteristics of childish thinking behind him. This suggests an image of educational development that is common: one in which the discontinuities between childish and adult thinking are prominent and considered most important. This view of education has, we think, hindered the perception of articulation of a coherent theory of educational development.

Childhood, immaturity, childish thinking, adolescence, are typically seen as things we grow *out of*. The notion of educational development we present here suggests rather that these be seen as things we grow *with* and *on*. It considers the continuities between childish and adult thinking much more significant than any discontinuities. It represents educational development as a process of *accumulation*, the characteristics of the stages not as things we grow out of but as things we elaborate on; not as things we discard on entering later stages but as things that become more disciplined and controlled.

So the stages are not to be seen as stages we pass through and leave behind. Each stage contributes something significant to the mature adult's manner of making sense of the world and human experience. That is, the ironic stage seems to be made of the accumulated contributions of the previous stages, all under the control of the key ironic perception outlined above.

Given the characterizations in the previous sections, what can we say is contributed by the mythic stage? The child, who is indeed father of the man, learns to project his inner mental images onto the world and so give human meaning to it. This mythic ability to connect the mind to the world seems fundamental to all later learning. However sophisticated thinking may become, and however well the mythic level is controlled by irony, the establishment of meaning requires the projection of mental forms onto the world and some basic effective orientation toward whatever particular knowledge is being dealt with. Though the adult may use many-termed systems to organize knowledge, still underlying these will be found those most basic binary opposites on which later thinking is elaborated — good/bad, fear/security, and so forth. The mythic stage, then, contributes the ability to derive human meaning from the inhuman world.

The romantic stage contributes the ability to inhabit imaginatively other times, places, and forms of living. It contributes to the adult a sense of vivacity, vitality, and buoyancy in dealing with the world. It contributes, in short, a sense of romance. However well irony keeps the adult's sense of romance in check, the ability to form romantic associations with knowledge is necessary to give energy and enthusiasm to learning. The lack of romance leads either to ignorant children or to knowledgeable pedantry.

The philosophic stage contributes the ability to search for the recurrent, the typical, for laws and patterns. It contributes the ability to organize knowledge into more generally meaningful schemes. If, at the philosophic stage these schemes tend to be out of control, dominating knowledge and inquiry inappropriately, once controlled by an ironic intelligence they become flexible servants, making visible a variety of ways of making sense of social, psychological, and historical processes, and of one's place and role as an agent or participant in them.

If ironic intelligence has a purpose that is different from the previous stages, how would it be described? Is it to be able to answer Pilate's ironic question, "What is truth?" in its own "ironic" way? And why should we want to do that? Knowing the truth, as Keats observed, provides humans with an aesthetic pleasure — the kind of joy that Nietzsche and Yeats have written about most articulately — that both motivates and justifies the search.

APPROACHING A THEORY

In the introduction of this chapter we claimed that the above four stages would lead us toward a theory of educational development, because they would focus on developmental phenomena of educational interest and use. Why should the kind of categories focused on be considered of more *educational* interest than those of, say, Piaget or Erik Erikson?

Let us for the moment assume that the above four stages do more or less accurately describe a common process of educational development within our culture. The categories focused on are of educational interest because they lead directly to principles for unit and lesson planning, because they lead to a general view of the educational process, because they are fertile in suggestions of potential educational significance, and because empirical testing of them would produce knowledge of educational interest. Each of these claims will be elaborated below, but it should be noted here that the last is the crucial sign of what *kind* of theory is being used.

First, an educational theory should lead to principles for unit and lesson planning. To take as an example the romantic stage: it suggests that for the most effective learning a unit or lesson should begin with something dramatic that is distant from the student's everyday experience but that involves some powerful transcendent quality with which the student may romantically associate. This beginning theme should set up an expectation that should then be developed or complicated, and there should be a clear ending that satisfies the original expectation. Within the unit there should be the opportunity to investigate some aspect in minutest detail. The middle and end should be concerned in some sense with an exploration of extremes or limits of the subject. Content, say in the sciences, may be more readily understood if presented not as objective established truths, but in the context of the life of whoever established those truths, as products of human genius, struggle, determination, and so forth. None of this necessitates falsification of whatever is to be taught. Rather it simply suggests principles for organizing knowledge to be most readily accessible at any particular stage.

An educational theory should present a general image of the whole process of educational development. Our lack of such images results in the dearth of *educational* theories. Our dominant image seems to be that of the "expanding horizons" curriculum model, derived from Dewey, where education is seen to begin with the child and everyday experience and gradually work outward to the rest of the world along lines of content associations. The image presented by our sketch is almost the opposite, and is much more plausible and coherent with common experience. These stages lead to an image of educational development that works from outside limits inward. The mythic stage ignores the restrictions of reality whenever convenient, proliferating impossible creatures and worlds that never existed, while elaborating basic categories of thinking; the romantic stage works to confine thought within reality while exploring its limits; the philosophic stage charts the general features of reality in more detail; and the ironic stage explores particulars for their own sake.

This general process seems to be repeated within each stage as well. Entry to a stage seems to involve engaging the most general characteristics of the stage and gradually refining them. For example, entry to the romantic stage involves engagement with the most extreme and bizarre aspects of reality, with newly felt sentiments largely out of control, with an insecure sense of where the limits of the real are; then these are gradually brought under greater control. Entry to the philosophic stage seems to involve generating the most crude and general scheme, which is then gradually refined and sophisticated. Entry to the ironic stage seems to involve a sudden grasp at a new manner of making sense of things that is initially general and vague and is gradually refined. In another context this initial move to an ironic stage has been called "alienating" irony; the sense of alienation following from letting go the philosophic general schemes and suddenly finding oneself adrift in a sea of particularity. It takes time and courage to establish orientation within the shifting world that is the lot of the ironic mind.

Entry to a stage, then, is not achieved by gradual development and mastery of its characteristics. The foundations of each stage are, indeed, developed during the previous stages, but the actual transitions come more like a sudden "vision," a sudden coalescence that creates a qualitatively different way of making sense of things. Reflecting on their own educational development, most people can remember such relatively sudden transitions. These changes are clearly crucial to educational development, but, like most important educational phenomena, have received very little attention because they are not brought into focus by non-educational theories of development.

This sketch suggests a potentially rich crop of educationally focused ideas. As one possibility, it brings the topic of "critical periods" to matters of educational significance. That is, it suggests the possibility that each stage represents the critical period for the development of the capacities characteristic of each stage. Such an hypothesis — granted that the description is accurate — is clearly educationally significant, and worthy of further exploration. Should it be found to be true it would be likely to have a profound effect on the typical curriculum.

The significance of all this rests on the assumption that the description is more or less accurate, that what is characterized does have some empirical referent and is not all an elaborate invention or piece of "objectified" autobiography. Whether it will be found worthy of elaboration and refinement, and empirical testing, will turn first on its *plausibility*, on how well it seems to cohere with readers' experience and observation and with available data.

But, given the present purpose, it will be sufficient if readers acknowledge that the kinds of phenomena dealt with in composing this sketch are appropriate for building an educational theory, a theory of educational development; that an elaborated theory based on these phenomena is more likely to be of educational use than the kind of psychological and sociological theories at present all too familiar to us in education.

As we have argued, and will elaborate further in chapter eight, a crucial difference between education and socialization is that in the latter case we know more or less clearly what our desired end product is to look like. Behavior then can be shaped toward prescribed ends. The prescriptions of an educational theory, however, have to allow for increasing variety, possibility, difference, as we move toward the desired end product. Indeed, success in the educational process requires that our product be different from any other educated person. Success in socialization comes when our product shares with the other members of a social group the qualities and skills, the knowledge and understanding that the process has been designed to develop. Given this fundamental difference, we might reasonably expect an educational theory to be quite different from those psychological and sociological theories that may serve the socialization process. This by itself hardly justifies a theory of the kind sketched above, but it should defend it against complaints that it is not like the kinds of psychological theories whose implications are supposed to guide educational practice.[13]

CHAPTER SIX

Teaching and Believing

THE DISTINCTION we have made between socializing and educating can be used to reflect on the merits of different approaches to moral education, or the teaching of ethical beliefs and principles. In this chapter we will contrast two approaches—one that is currently very much present in the debates over the rightful place of ethics in the schools, and another that we would like to propose as an alternative. We will describe the first only briefly because so much has already been written about it under the familiar title of values clarification.[1] The second approach needs a more detailed explanation because it is less widely known.

The values clarification approach to moral education is not so much education as it is socialization in the ways one can learn to express beliefs in values, whatever those values may be, and to suppress conflict over values. The criteria for a succesful program in values clarification are basically the criteria of socialization. The general point is to encourage each individual to declare a favored position with regard to a specified forced-choice moral situation that requires a solution, and then to suppress the conflict among individuals that comes about because chosen solutions are in conflict.

Conflict is not so much confronted as it is dealt away with on grounds that there is no way to decide whose position or whose principles are ultimately more or less right, more or less moral. The answer to a conflict of values is to consider it unimportant because unresolvable in theory. The ultimate right in this program of moral socialization is the right to hold whatever value beliefs one cares to hold, so long as one holds them openly and consistently. The means used to elicit personal statements about values is akin to the means Dewey favored in social studies instruction, that is, confronting problems that may or do occur in familiar social conditions and solving these problems in ways that satisfy some criteria of practical utility.

In this approach, coming up with a decision or solution is central and decisions are made individually. No individual decision can be judged superior or inferior by appeal to more general ethical principles or standards. The aim of such a program is to encourage individuals to clarify their own values, not to change them; to see valuing as a highly personal matter, not as a matter of subjecting personal opinions to the rigorous tests of rational and ethical scrutiny in order to make them conform more closely with a higher standard of ethical thinking.

We have no objection to the clarification of held beliefs—in fact this is the starting point of the alternative approach we now describe — but we do object to the failure of such a program to make this experience educative. We encourage the open discussion of values and ethical beliefs in schools at all levels, from the primary grades through college, and we also encourage the study of our culture's rich literature, produced by some of the best and most noble minds in history, on these very same values and beliefs. Such discussion and the literature that records it represent a view of human experience that transcends the parochial limitations of any particular set of socializing conditions. Not to extend values clarification into an exploration of this magnificent history of moral philosophy is a travesty of education.

It is a good idea, for purposes of socialization, to plan a discussion of what obligation each individual owes to the society of which he or she is a part. This can easily be done by inventing a hypothetical example of a common, familiar conflict between a social good and an individual's self-interest (when it is justified for a hungry man to steal bread?). The ensuing discussion of such a question could be very lively and useful for bringing out differences in feeling and reasoning. But it would be sad for the students' *education* not to bring in Plato's account of Socrates' refusal to escape his own death sentence — unjust though it was—and not to talk about the moral basis of his refusal in contrast to other possible bases.

We offer this example as only one way to extend a socializing activity into an educative experience. There are, of course, many other ways to make such a transformation. The difference lies in going beyond the immediate, personal, hypothetical, and ahistorical focus on clarifying values, to expose students to a very important part of the Western heritage. We think everyone deserves to learn who Socrates was and we think it would be educationally, morally, and politically good if everyone—not just liberal arts majors in college—struggled to understand the circumstances of his death. What happened in Athens two thousand years ago still matters. The way Plato expressed his account of what happened still matters. It enriches one's view of values and obligation to learn what happened — and that in turn contributes to one's education.

THE INEVITABILITY OF HOLDING PHILOSOPHICAL BELIEFS, OR LE BOURGEOIS UNDERGRADUATE GENTILHOMME

The title of this section comes from Molière's comedy, *Le Bourgeois Gentilhomme*, in which M. Jourdain is taught by the philosophy master that he has in fact been speaking "prose" all his life without knowing that it was "prose." The philosophy master, being in M. Jourdain's employ, was tactfully laconic in his witness of this revelation, while *le monsieur* fell agape in pride and wonder.

Philosophy masters these days rarely have the luxury of such tutorial arrangements with their students. Many of us who teach philosophy find ourselves dealing with groups of students, young and old, whose diverse motivations *vis-à-vis* philosophy make it difficult to know just how best to begin teaching a given class, and make it nearly impossible to get satisfaction from teaching in the lecture/text fashion. The problems that concern us here are those of introducing philosophy (1) to students who may be motivated to take the course only by a program requirement and therefore may hold a skeptical reluctance toward philosophy as a whole, and (2) to students who may indeed be curious to know more about philosophy but who may also feel intimidated by its erudite and esoteric reputation. Our dealing with these problems has led us to develop a "belief profile" concept, a sample section of which is given in figure 6.1.

Many teachers have noticed two things that *must* affect their teaching styles. First, the number of students who want to study something in particular is quite small compared with the number of students who do not know what else to do for the moment. Second, from under this motley student mantle comes a demand to explain what philosophy of all things has to do with anything important, such as getting a job.

One must accept the sundry character of our student bodies, and accept the burden of explanation demanded. One must spend hours—too many hours — trying to justify the calamity of "having to take
(Continued on page 83)

FIGURE 6.1

Danyberg Belief Profile: Ethics

Please indicate your response to <u>each</u> item by checking the part of the scale that corresponds to your present belief.

strongly agree	somewhat agree	slightly agree	neutral	slightly disagree	somewhat disagree	strongly disagree

1. There is essentially no difference between "factual" statements and "value" statements.

   _____ _____ _____ _____ _____ _____ _____

2. Anything that is "good" is also "right."

   _____ _____ _____ _____ _____ _____ _____

3. Anything that is "right" is also "good."

   _____ _____ _____ _____ _____ _____ _____

4. A "value" judgment is also a "moral" judgment.

   _____ _____ _____ _____ _____ _____ _____

5. It is possible to find a criterion for determining the "validity" of ethical judgments.

   _____ _____ _____ _____ _____ _____ _____

6. Value statements such as "Democracy is good and communism is bad" are really <u>commands</u> that mean "you should choose democracy over communism."

   _____ _____ _____ _____ _____ _____ _____

7. One cannot deduce an "ought" statement from a series of "is" statements (e.g., man is a rational animal, so man ought to act rationally).

   _____ _____ _____ _____ _____ _____ _____

8. There is such a thing, or quality, as "intrinsic" good.

   _____ _____ _____ _____ _____ _____ _____

9. It is possible to make moral judgments that apply to all people.

   _____ _____ _____ _____ _____ _____ _____

10. It is possible to make moral judgments that apply to one person at all times.

_____ _____ _____ _____ _____ _____ _____

11. If one "senses" an obligation, one "has" an obligation.

_____ _____ _____ _____ _____ _____ _____

12. Intuition is the best source for moral judgments.

_____ _____ _____ _____ _____ _____ _____

13. Revelation is the best source for moral judgments.

_____ _____ _____ _____ _____ _____ _____

14. Rational thinking is the best source for moral judgments.

_____ _____ _____ _____ _____ _____ _____

15. Empirical or scientific data are the best source for moral judgments.

_____ _____ _____ _____ _____ _____ _____

16. "Science" is no more related to "morality" than is blacksmithing.

_____ _____ _____ _____ _____ _____ _____

17. Everything in the world has ethical aspects and implications.

_____ _____ _____ _____ _____ _____ _____

18. "Morality" is a function of convention, not nature.

_____ _____ _____ _____ _____ _____ _____

19. "Good triumphs over evil"; therefore, what survives, what is strongest, is "good."

_____ _____ _____ _____ _____ _____ _____

20. It is not possible that one who really understands what is "good" could then choose to do bad or evil.

_____ _____ _____ _____ _____ _____ _____

21. It is not possible that pain can ever be thought of as a "good."

_____ _____ _____ _____ _____ _____ _____

FIGURE 6.1 *(continued)*

22. If I can decide the question "What should I do?" I can also then decide the question "What should you do?"

_____ _____ _____ _____ _____ _____ _____

23. An act can be "wrong" and "good."

_____ _____ _____ _____ _____ _____ _____

24. There is essentially no difference between deciding what is hot, hotter, hottest, and deciding what is good, better, best.

_____ _____ _____ _____ _____ _____ _____

25. It is impossible to understand the term "guilt" without first understanding the term "ought."

_____ _____ _____ _____ _____ _____ _____

26. There exists a "level of being" higher than human life which is the "real" source of morality.

_____ _____ _____ _____ _____ _____ _____

27. What we call "morality" is at the bottom no more than a desire, or choice to believe this rather than that; one can change one's "morality" merely by changing one's mind.

_____ _____ _____ _____ _____ _____ _____

28. There can be no "morality" that is not "just."

_____ _____ _____ _____ _____ _____ _____

29. Man invented the concept of "justice"; there is no example of "justice" to be found in "nature."

_____ _____ _____ _____ _____ _____ _____

30. "Evil" means the same as "bad."

_____ _____ _____ _____ _____ _____ _____

philosophy," because philosophy is perceived as something of a contentless discipline which now ridicules the poets of our culture instead of inspiring them as it once did—in *some* cultures anyway, if not in an earlier version of the North American. As philosophy is perceived more as a discipline than as a disposition, as "knowledge" is seen to be more of a function of "proof" than of "belief," as the literature of the field becomes more mechanically numerable and symbolic, to this extent it becomes onerous to entice students into the study of philosophy, to amuse students with its charm, or to make the case that philosophy is for people generally and not for professionals only.

We are not so much interested to cant a new slogan of "Philosophy to the People" as we are interested to demonstrate that philosophy, or at least some philosophical belief, is inevitably present in the lives of thinking persons, that the primary problems of philosophy can be stated in such a way as to show that they are also the primary problems of living. As Michael Scriven puts it: "We cannot choose whether to answer [these problems], for to live requires that we answer them in our lives. We can only choose whether to think about them."[2]

PHILOSOPHY AND PERSONALITY

Socrates learned that knowing oneself was the foundation of philosophy, and he expanded this learning into the claim that the unexamined life is not worth living. Oedipus led some of us to believe that the well-examined life is often unlivable. And not too long ago John Barth suggested that self-knowledge is almost always bad news. These three, together, give us a way to think about neophyte philosophizing: whatever one knows about oneself is at least part of what one knows about philosophy. Fichte suggested that the kind of philosophy one chooses depends upon the kind of person one is, and this suggests that philosophy does not really change the person so much as the person's living changes his philosophy. Nietzsche, as usual, put it more fetchingly: "Gradually it has become clear to me what every great philosophy so far has been: namely, the personal confession of its author and a kind of involuntary and unconscious memoir [autobiography]."[3]

Each of us has a biography; that much is clear. It is not so clear that one's biography has in it a philosophy of sorts. It is, however, at least plausible that if one were to learn a certain manner of expressing certain aspects of autobiography, it would become evident to what extent one had been developing philosophical positions on philosophical issues.

In attempting such expression, as the Belief Profile is meant to facilitate, we find out a good deal about beliefs that we have held, with or without conscious awareness. We also learn about some of the implicit difficulties we have in justifying such beliefs, and in expressing them clearly enough to be understood by another person who may or may not share them. Such a focus on one's held beliefs is intrinsically interesting: there is no more favorite topic of conversation than oneself.

Now some may object that although this exercise may be of value to philosophers, it simply is not appropriate to expect students to express their own philosophical beliefs and their own justifications for these beliefs. To begin with, goes this argument, they lack the skills necessary for philosophical analysis of beliefs and their justifications. What's more, we should remember that such philosophizing often involves more sophistication and more ability to cope with grand-scale conceptual reorientations than we can or even ought to expect of most students.

There surely is a point to this objection, but not a clearly productive one. If we sustain the objection we have no alternative other than to introduce our students to philosophy through the beliefs held by *others*, and we are then led, by their usefulness for such purposes, to texts of the he-said-this-and-she-said-that variety, which, in their second-hand (often third-hand) and compendious character, are not immediately compelling to the fundamentally unmotivated reader. We remain obliged to *provide* such motivation where it does not exist, and that has been the baleful, boring bane of textbook teachers everywhere.

If, however, we choose not to sustain the objection, we might appeal to G. E. Moore's way of doing philosophy as a model for our point of view. As G. J. Warnock puts it:

> Part of the great interest and importance of [the way Moore did philosophy] is that this is something anyone can do — to practice philosophy in the manner of Moore, it is not necessary to have (as most of us doubtless have not) nor pretend to have (as some at least would be unwilling to do) large-scale metaphysical anxieties. It is necessary only to want to get things clear.[4]

Now getting clear on where our living has led us, in terms of the beliefs we have come to hold, with varying degrees of conscious awareness, is what our proposal for teaching philosophy is meant to assist. One thing we can be sure a student brings to class is his or her own biography. The task is to help, maieutically, its expression in terms of held beliefs.

THE PSYCHOLOGY OF PERSONAL CONSTRUCTS

In the view of Professor J. P. Corbett:

The work of philosophical education must begin by raising radical doubts. The teacher must apply his energy and skill to throwing the convictions of his student into disarray. He must personify the malignant demon of Descartes and stir up every doubt he can. This is the only way in which accepted principles of validity can be dredged up to the surface of the mind for examination. But principles of validity do not rest inside a personality, detached from the emotions and the will. They are an integral part of the personality; they are, in a very real sense, what a man is and how he lives.[5]

This dredging up of one's "principles of validity" is very like what George Kelly suggests in his psychology of personal constructs when he says we can explore the subjective maps that people chart to deal with the psychological terrain of their lives. Or, in a slightly different way, we can understand that "man looks at his world through transparent patterns or templets which he creates and then attempts to fit over the realities of which the world is composed."[6]

We anticipate an objection at this point over the fact that Kelly is a psychotherapist and that teaching philosophy is not psychotherapy, whatever else is may be. Besides, a philosopher or a philosophy teacher is not trained for therapeutics and therefore should not act therapeutically, or deal directly with the personality. For the sake of getting on with a discussion of the Belief Profile, we will not dispute this objection by arguing over the relations between teaching and therapy, among learning, healing, and health. We will instead sustain the objection on the grounds that one can deal with another's beliefs, some of which can be likened to "principles of validity," some to "subjective maps," some to "templets," which are created constructs meant to help interpret the world, without assuming a therapeutic role or frame of mind, but solely through the use of a diagnostic instrument designed to yield a profile of existing, held beliefs. Before discussing the Profile itself, however, we would like to elaborate just briefly Kelly's theory of personal constructs because the theory has been of significant influence in the development of the Profile.

Kelly's psychology of personal constructs is of a category in the field of personality studies called "phenomenological theory," a category that embraces the theories of Kurt Lewin, Carl Rogers, Gordon Allport, Frederick Perls, and perhaps R. D. Laing, as well as Kelly. The theories of this category are normally contrasted with Type and Trait theories (Sheldon, Cattell, Guilford, Eysenck, and sometimes Jung), with Psychodynamic theories (Freud, Jung, Fromm, Erikson, Adler, Sullivan, Horney, Dollard and Miller), and with Social Behavior theories (Watson, Skinner, Bandura, and perhaps Glasser).

In contrast to psychodynamic theory wherein *motive* and *unconscious conflict* are, respectively, the prime units and process, Kelly's emphasis is on a person's own constructs, or categories or templets, which one uses to sort out the important from the matter-of-fact, in order to exercise some degree of control over events that affect one's life. The critical elements of the theory are these:

1. People perceive and construe behavior, and they generate abstractions about themselves and others.
2. These perceptions-turned-abstractions are called constructs. They act as patterns or templets for interpreting experience.
3. All people are like scientists in that they generate hypotheses and constructs that help them anticipate, predict, and control events in the world with which they are involved.
4. One way a person tries to improve his constructs, to give them a better "fit," is to subsume them with superordinate constructs or systems, which are, for the most part, systems of belief.
5. A major presupposition of the theory is that "all of our present interpretations of the universe are subject to revision or replacement." (Although each of us has, inevitably, a biography, we are not inevitably *victims* of that biography.)
6. Sometimes we hesitate to experiment with our construct systems because we fear the ambiguity that may result if we lose the ability to predict and control.
7. A person is not necessarily articulate about the constructs and construct (or belief) systems he places on the world.
8. A superordinate construct has a deterministic control over its elements, but the elements do not determine the constructs used to subsume them. A person, then, to the extent that he can construe his circumstances, can free himself from their domination. A man can enslave himself, but he can free himself also by reconstruing his life, or parts of it.

9. The concern of the psychologist or psychotherapist is the utility of the constructs in question, not their truth; the object of therapy is to provide conditions for the person to elaborate and test for implications his own operating set of constructs, or beliefs, which is to say, controls. In light of new experience they may be modified.

BELIEF CONSTRUCTS AND BELIEF PROFILES

What Kelly calls a superordinate construct or system is very like Kenneth Boulding's notion of "social image"[7] through which we filter messages that we call knowledge. Another conceptual similarity worth noting here is the one between J. P. Corbett's "principles of validity," which are "what a man is and how he lives," and W. V. Quine's view of believing as a "disposition to respond in certain ways when the appropriate issue arises."[8]

Now, insofar as holding a philosophical view can be likened to holding a superordinate construct or system (consciously or not, articulated or not), or a social image of knowledge, or a set of validity principles, or that disposition called believing, and insofar as these aspects of human living are *inevitable* constituents of one's own biography, then holding a philosophical view is *inevitable*, whether one has been instructed in philosophy and its refinements or not. Insofar as one has construed personal experience, abstracted some of these constructs, appealed to principles of validity in the course of daily living, and been disposed toward believing, one has been "speaking philosophy" just as surely as M. Jourdain had been "speaking prose" those forty years before he knew what to call it.

Assuming that we all do have, in the lines of our own biographies, beliefs on philosophical issues, we still have the question of what a paper and pencil Profile has to do with them. In our experience instruments, devices, machines and the like devised to increase the economy of some aspect of human affairs (in this case introducing students to philosophy) have in them inherent invitations to superficial thinking. Jacob Burckhardt predicted from his century that our century would be one of "great simplifiers," tempting us away from complexity and toward the essence of tyranny. We do not wish the Belief Profile to be understood or used as a great simplifier.

John Dewey held that the most pervasive fallacy of philosophic thinking is the neglect of context. Such neglect takes two forms. One is the *analytic fallacy*, wherein distinctions and elements that are discriminated are treated as if they were final and self-sufficient (leading to various forms of atomistic particularism). The other is the *fallacy of unlimited extension or universalization,* wherein distinctions and elements that are discriminated are lost altogether when the contextual limitations under which such discrimination takes place are ignored in the metaphysically anxious rush for coherence and unity.[9] Any instrument designed to represent the views or beliefs of persons is subject to both of these fallacies which are two of philosophy's great simplifiers. We hope to avoid charges of yielding to these wily invitations to fallacy by stipulating some limits of use for the Belief Profile.

1. It is meant only to be used as an aid in deciding how specifically to introduce beginning students to philosophy.
2. It is not to be thought of as a summary of any one philosopher's views, nor of a student's beliefs in a given area, nor of the area itself. It is merely an indicator of likely connections between a student's held beliefs on a given issue and a recognized philosopher's held beliefs on the same issue.
3. It is not to be used as an evaluative examination.
4. It is not to be used as a text or syllabus substitute.
5. It is not to be used as a substitute for teacher-student conferences and dialogue; it is to be used to promote and prepare for conferences and dialogue, and perhaps debate.

The application of the Belief Profile would go something like this: (a) at the start of a class or of a unit of a class, the student marks, for example, the ethics section of the Profile according to instructions; (b) the teacher checks each Profile for clusters of "Strongly Agree" and "Strongly Disagree" items; (c) the teacher compares these belief clusters with a reference list coded to match the numbered items of the Profile; (d) on the basis of this comparison the teacher recommends a selected bit of reading calculated either to give the student an experience of seeing his own beliefs stated in the words of a *bona fide* philosopher or to confront the student with a succinct statement supporting an opposite or at least conflicting point of view; (e) the student does the suggested reading and reports his reaction to the teacher. This in turn provides the teacher with some immediate feedback as to how well he is "reading" the student's beliefs, how well he is matching or challenging those beliefs, and what the next step in the process might be.[10]

Two assumptions lurk beneath this application description.

First, we are assuming that students will be at least surprised if not pleased or even flattered to find that they think somewhat like a philosopher, or that they have thought about philosophical issues and questions already. Second, we are assuming that such a reaction will breed a certain motivation, by virtue of association with a model, a philosopher, that would otherwise not have shown itself—at least not so soon. If these two assumptions hold, the question, "What does philosophy have to do with me, or with real life?" will have been answered by an actual demonstration of such a connection.

This approach to teaching ethics is consistent with our view of education in contrast to socialization. It incorporates an emphasis on the personal nature of learning with an emphasis on extending personal experience into an acquaintance with the record of philosophical thought in our culture. It does not aim at group consensus, nor is it satisfied with mere public expression of any held values. It leads the student, and the teacher, into the lasting conversation on the subjects of "right" and "good" that is near the heart of philosophy itself—a conversation that serves as the educational link between generations.

CHAPTER SEVEN

Beliefs and the Educational Curriculum

FOR THE COMPOSER of the socializing curriculum there is a referent available to which appeal can be made in order to justify the inclusion or omission of some activity. That referent is obviously not simple and unambiguous—it is the complex society into which the student is to be initiated. Nor is it just the society as it exists, but reference may also be made to likely future forms of the society. Our beliefs and desires about the direction of social change will thus form a part of our referent.

While we are socializing students to be able to deal with a social world that does not yet exist, our ideals have to be constrained by reasonable extrapolations from present social forms. As argued in chapter three, our educational theory, too, may likely involve educating students to conform with some ideal never yet achieved. The referent, then, for the composer of the educational curriculum will be an educational theory. That theory needs to be constrained by what we know to be logically and psychologically possible.

The constraints on the composer of the socializing curriculum are clearly quite different from those on the composer of the educational curriculum, and the criteria each refers to in order to decide on the relative value of activities that compete for time and space in the two curricula are different. Put simply, one may say that the referent available to the composer of socializing curriculum is firmer. Consequently, in times when there is pressure to justify activities in schools on clearly firmer bases, the socializing curriculum will likely gain ground against the educational curriculum.

The referent available to the composer of the educational curriculum — an educational theory — needs as constituents a set of presuppositions. The composer of the socializing curriculum also carries a set of presuppositions into his task, but the weaker empirical constraints on the educational curriculum's composer ensure that the realm of beliefs or presuppositions plays a more significant part. Thus discussions about the educational curriculum should allow for the relatively large part played by beliefs or presuppositions, and we should adopt appropriate strategies in our arguments and decision-making.

This chapter exposes rather crudely something of the range of influence of presuppositions in composing the educational curriculum and then discusses appropriate strategies for dealing with educational decisions in light of the influential role of presuppositions. The initial exposure is crude in that an exhaustive mapping of presuppositions is not attempted, nor are they dealt with in any particular order or level of generality. All that is aimed for in the first part of the chapter is a sense of the very great influence that presuppositions have in composing the educational curriculum.

HUMAN NATURE: GOOD/BAD?

A few words first about this and the following subheadings: the most simple, not to say crude, terms are used to indicate the presuppositions that are characterized. Clearly, few people hold the simplistic position that human nature is either absolutely good or bad, or even try to make a rational assessment of the trustworthiness of human nature in general. But these bald terms are used to suggest a continuum along which a range of presuppositions about human nature can be located.

One of the most powerful influences on our curriculum decisions is our subtly and subconsciously formed presupposition about how good, reliable, trustworthy—or the opposite—human nature is. The presupposition that human nature is typically good leads to the belief that people will incline to do good if unconstrained—"good" being used here for whatever one approves of: pro-human behavior generally or the learning of physics in particular. Thus people who hold this presupposition tend to blame environmental conditions, formal constraints, or institutions for any "bad" that occurs—whether it be anti-human behavior, or failure to learn Physics or reading or whatever subject. With regard to curriculum, this presupposition leads to the range of positions that favor lack of constraint on children and trust in their instincts. That is, if children will move *naturally* toward the good, and if to learn Physics and reading is good then, if not prevented by some external condition, they will choose naturally to learn those things of most value to them.

Holding this presupposition leads to feeling no sense of risk or danger in removing constraints and providing greater freedom. Indeed, quite the reverse—change and innovation are favored, almost regardless of the kind of changes, not just because they may involve the removal of constraints but because they provide moments when the freedom for "good" human nature to express itself is at a maximum. Even innovations designed to provide greater freedom tend to become formalized and rigid, so it is the freedom involved between the breaking up of one structure and the closing in of another that is most highly valued—and so more or less constant change tends to be preferred. Rigid classroom formats, traditional teaching methods, structures and formalities of all kinds are thus seen as barriers preventing natural goodness from being exercised. "Free schools," "open education," even de-schooling will tend to be supported — supported with confidence that education will naturally improve because of the reduction of constraints. Student-initiated inquiry and open-ended project work will be preferred to teacher domination and prescribed closed-ended tasks.

The person who presupposes that human nature is bad is led to see traditional forms, institutions, and constraints as carefully built defenses *against* the exercise of a naturally destructive, ignorance-preferring human nature. Consequently, periods of change and innovation are seen as times of high risk at which it is only too easy to lose far more than may be gained. With regard to curriculum, this presupposition leads to the desire to defend all institutions and forms that achieve any degree of success, however small, in teaching and controlling children. This sense of institutional constraints, being important defenses against people's natural inclination to the "bad," leads to a particularly strong feeling that quite severe constraints and pressures are justified and required to ensure that children master those skills society needs for its continuance and that they recreate in themselves the culture that has taken millennia of effort to make. It is obvious that these general feelings will lead to programs more or less the opposite of those indicated above.

It may help to clarify this continuum if extreme positions at either end are sketched, and then the middle position. The extreme left presupposes that human nature is so good that all constraints and institutions should be immediately removed or destroyed. Nothing can be lost in throwing out all curriculum guides, classroom structures, formal courses and disciplines, even teaching and schools, because only in the absence of these constraints will the natural goodness of the child find free flower. And if this freedom fails to produce the basic skills necessary for the continuance of society, so much the worse for society: this only shows what an artificial, inhuman, and stifling set of institutions it is. The "rightmost" extreme is led to see humans as evil animals, whose civilization is an incredibly frail structure holding in control the human bestiality that threatens to overwhelm civilized life at every turn. All change is resisted because no possible change could be worth what is put at risk.

The person in the middle of this continuum presupposes that human nature is neither good nor bad, or perhaps that human nature is in some circumstances likely to produce good, in others, bad. This leads to the desire to provide some structural defenses against the bad but to leave sufficient flexibility so that the good might have some room for exercise. If at the far right no change is acceptable and at the far left any change is desirable, readiness to accept changes in the middle will be qualified by the requirement that either evidence or good reasons be given that the changes will lead to improvements.

Other continua of presuppositions about human nature lead to equally diverse positions. People have, for example, differing presuppositions about the plasticity or flexibility of human nature. This leads to different positions on the extent to which teaching may be effective. This range of presuppositions underlies the nature/nurture or environmentalist/geneticist disputes. Let the above suffice, however, as an indication of how different presuppositions about human nature lead to different positions on some curriculum issues.

CULTURE: WITHIN/WITHOUT?

This second set of presuppositions is rather nearer the surface of typical conscious reflection than the first. Overt arguments about curriculum, however, rarely try to locate where the arguers think culture lies. This location is important because presuppositions about where culture is determine people's views of what it is and, consequently, what role it has in the curriculum.

If one presupposes that culture is "without," one conceives of it as somehow contained in, or composed of, objects—the products of great minds: books, pictures, theatrical performances, music, and so forth—associated with a set of feelings and attitudes. These cultural objects and the appropriate feelings and attitudes about them exist in a publicly determined hierarchy of value. Education thus becomes the process of making children familiar with the hierarchy of cultural objects and internalizing the public standards of evaluation and appreciation of them. This leads to seeing the curriculum as largely a curriculum of content and education as a process of acculturation upward in the various hierarchies. The cultural objects are seen as of permanent value and meaning unaffected by the current situation. Indeed, their value cannot change because they are fixed standards of value against which present experience, products, and events may be measured.

This presupposition leads to a curriculum in which authority is important—both the authority of culture itself, which the child must absorb to become, as it were, fully human, and of the teacher as the representative or, better, embodiment of the public standards that must be learned. The curriculum will be highly structured to ensure the child's proper development upwards in the various hierarchies. Since access to the best cultural products requires mastery of a considerable range of knowledge and skills, the curriculum will involve pressure for achievement, and will frequently test to ensure that each step has been taken successfully. The value that will result from this mastery will be more important than any discomfort, distress, or even suffering that may result from pressure in the process.

(Authoritarian attitudes tend to follow from the presupposition that culture is "without"; however, they need not. Similarly this presupposition tends to be associated with the presupposition that human nature is bad; but again, it need not. It is, for example, possible for someone who presupposes that human nature is good to presuppose that culture is "without"—in which case that person would be led to believe that if children are left largely to their own devices they will naturally come to internalize the public hierarchy of values and appropriately appreciate cultural objects. The more common combination, however, is for the person who presupposes human nature to be good, to presuppose culture to be "within.")

The person who presupposes culture is "within" is led to see it as a set of experiences, not objects. The quality of a book, for example, is not measured in terms of any public standard, but simply by its effect on the individual reader. The hierarchy of cultural values is thus composed by each individual for him/herself, and this hierarchy is considered autonomous. Shakespeare, then, might move one person profoundly and be no part of the culture of someone else; and no value comparisons can be made between individuals' cultures, and there can be no sense in which one should work to get from some object the same kind of experience someone else gets. Public standards or claims about the cultural value of objects are considered largely meaningless — at best a guide to things worth trying. Those who presuppose that culture is "within" will talk about many cultures; those who believe culture is "without" will talk of only one objective culture. There can be no such thing as a counter-culture or alternate-cultures; there is simply culture and varying degrees of ignorance or participation in it.

The extremes of this continuum may be represented on the right by the person who is led to see culture as residing entirely in a strictly organized hierarchy of objects — so that one could, as it were, buy culture by buying objects of publicly accepted cultural value, the higher up the hierarchy, the higher the price. To the left, the extreme presupposition leads to believing that what goes on inside one's head is the source and provides the standard of cultural value, regardless of its source or content. Thus drugs or push-penny can be considered equivalent to Beethoven's quartets if they produce the same degree of intense feeling.

This continuum of presuppositions determines profoundly curriculum issues such as are summed up by labels *process v. product*, or *intrinsic v. instrumental*. If one presupposes that culture is "within," it is the process one goes through in learning that is important. No future product is more important than present experience because the present experience *is* culture. The experience in classrooms must be of intrinsic value in the present. Toward the right of the continuum the process is seen merely as the means to this end, of little importance by itself. What is important is the achievement of internalizing the public standards.

CONSCIOUSNESS: PAST/PRESENT/FUTURE?

Societies and individuals vary in the way they make sense of experience with regard to the flow of time. Three basic positions may be characterized, as indicated by this subheading. Obviously no one locates his consciousness exclusively in the past or present or future; we combine them in varying degrees, though we tend to accentuate one or two at the expense of the other(s). B. A. van Groningen's characterizations will be used here:

> One person unsuspectingly gives all his attention to the direct present and tries to adapt himself to it with all its delights or sorrows. Another prefers to concentrate on the things which are

expected to happen; as a man of the future he is wrapped up in expectations, hope and fear; to him the present, even in its broadest aspect, is above all an approach, a prelude to coming events. There is still a third attitude, the one of the man who is strongly tied down to the past, who finds there the real values of life and who sees the present mainly as a result of that past; recollections and experience are more to him than expectations, he draws his vital energy from the past, borrows his convictions from it, and finds his bearings there.[1]

Clearly this set of presuppositions overlaps in various ways with some of those above, but there is a range of curriculum concerns that is particularly determined by this location of consciousness in time. One way of initially characterizing these is by showing how they influence attitudes toward History in the curriculum.

For the person who is predominantly past-conscious, History is important because knowledge of the past is responsible for securing our very identity; we are what we are and the world is what it is because of what happened in the past. To mix metaphors, it is both the anchor that provides security and the compass that guides us through times of rapid change—the more rapid the changes, the more important History is for stability and sound judgment. The past-conscious person will favor a curriculum that not only gives a central place to traditional academic History but also organizes all other subjects on a historical basis. Physics, for example, should be taught by introducing the child to Greek ideas of Physics; Alexandrian, medieval, Renaissance, Enlightenment, nineteenth-century, and, finally, modern should follow. This presupposition tends to lead to accepting that ontogeny recapitulates phylogeny in the mastery of knowledge and ideas.

To the present-conscious, History is of value in so far as it provides a direct enlightenment on current issues. Thus, most History before the nineteenth century is considered simply irrelevant to the needs of modern children. Our identity is not seen as formed by history, but is seen in terms of current social forms, institutions, ideologies. Teachers who are present-conscious collapse History to Social Studies and attempt to introduce children directly into the way the world is and works now. Thus while the past-conscious would prefer to teach children about the Greeks, the present-conscious would prefer to introduce them to the idea of democracy and take them out to see a local council working. It is presupposed by the present-conscious person that the children will gain a better understanding of their world from, say, a study of the make-up of a local shopping center than a study of Greek or Roman history. Urban or Environmental Studies will thus be preferred to the study of History.

To the future-conscious the study of History is totally irrelevant except insofar as it can indicate some trend that may be extrapolated into the future. Identity is composed of expectations. Future-ology would replace History in this person's curriculum, because it is the future, whose shape can be more or less inferred from present trends, that gives meaning and guidance to the present. The future-conscious teacher is led to prefer a curriculum that will prepare children for what is likely to happen, and so should not, in a period of rapid change like ours, concentrate on content (who can know what content will be appropriate to the requirements of the future?) but on encouraging flexibility rather than acquisition of knowledge, thinking-skills rather than things to think about, openness to change rather than commitment to a set of ideas and institutions.

Most readers are no doubt familiar with the extremes of each of the above positions: the dry pedant hostile to anything that is not at least a few centuries old, the narrow and ignorant activist, and the mindless "trendy."

The presuppositions reflected in these locations of consciousness in time do not affect only History. History is used as an example simply because their effect on its role in the curriculum is quite clear. But all elements of the curriculum are affected by these presuppositions.

CENTER OF VALUE: BODY/MIND/SOUL?

As with the previous suppositions, we rarely find a person who exclusively values the body or mind or soul at the absolute expense of the others. However, we do find a considerable variation in emphasis. Again, the subheading is very crude, so a few lines will be spent in characterizing people who are imbalanced quite heavily toward each of these centers of value, and the curriculum positions influenced by each presupposition will be briefly noted.

The person who presupposes that the body is of predominant value sees it as the source of sensation and sees sensation as the predominant form of gratification. The body is not simply an instrument that carries the mind about and needs to be fed, clothed and locomoted; it is, rather, the source whereby great pleasure may be derived, from feeding it, from decorating it, from its ability to move well and powerfully in sports or risky adventures. Ideas are of small importance; it is the sensuousness of music, painting, sculpture that represents their central value. The mind-centered person values ideas above all else, gets greatest gratification from the working of the mind. Since we are more familiar with this attitude in education we need not dwell on it. The soul-centered values the mystical, that is, that dimension of experience in which we locate our sense of awe, of mystery. For some it comes from contemplating the very fact of existence and for others it is in a set of beliefs about a world other than ours that guides them toward mystical experience; for some it is in the sense of the numinous behind appearances and for others it is in love. The extremes are familiar enough so as not to need characterizing.

With regard to the curriculum, the body-centered favors activities that lead to sensuous appreciation or physical activity or both. The mind-centered favors a curriculum that engages interest in ideas and leads to their valuing and skill in using them. The soul-centered strives for a curriculum that will constantly lead children beyond the prosaic world of factual knowledge, intellectual skills, and sensuous appreciation, to a sense of the mystery and wonder of things. Without going into more detail, it will be evident that people who presuppose one of these value centers to be of greater value than the others will conflict with people who hold one of the alternative presuppositions on a range of curriculum issues.

"MAKE PEOPLE LIKE ME!"

Underlying all the above presuppositions, or perhaps constituted by them, is a complex of presuppositions crudely summarized in this subheading. Underlying most curriculum decisions by any person lies the usually subconscious calculation of what will more likely lead toward children being made like him or her. Our immediate impulse is to reject such a crudely phrased claim, especially as it refers to ourselves—though it does seem to have some truth when it refers to our opponents.

If one examines the stated aims of even the most sophisticated educational thinkers one will find curricula clearly designed to produce people like their proposers. That is, the unstated aim that underlies those stated, and the most important and persistent of their aims, is to create curricula that will produce people like them. As educators, we may say that usually this is qualified by our desire to have a curriculum that will produce people like us, but without our "warts" — those deficiencies or faults we feel able to acknowledge.

Our decisions about curriculum are largely determined by the desire to produce people like our idealized image of ourselves.

Consider briefly some of the statements of aims or principles for a curriculum expressed by Dewey, Whitehead, Maritain, and Peters in William K. Frankena's collection, *Philosophy of Education*.[2] Dewey wants a product marked by "executive competency . . . by sociability . . . by aesthetic taste . . . trained intellectual method . . . [sensitivity] to the rights of others."[3] Whitehead wants the product of his curriculum "to experience the joy of discovery . . . see that general ideas give an understanding of the stress of events that pour through . . . life," to prove ideas, evoke curiosity, judgment and the "power of mastering a complicated tangle of circumstances, the use of theory in giving foresight in special cases," and to have, above all, "style."[4] Maritain wants "the conquest of internal and spiritual freedom to be achieved by the individual person, or, in other words, his liberation through knowledge and wisdom, good will, and love." He thinks that "no one is freer, or more independent than the one who gives himself for a cause or a real being worthy of the gift."[5] Peters' priorities include "sensitivity, a critical mind, respect for people and facts," and "a rationally held and intelligently applied moral code," so that children will "enter the Palace of Reason through the courtyard of Habit and Tradition."[6]

Our philosophers are writing about themselves. To state aims or principles for curriculum construction is a kind of covert autobiography, projecting outward into a different form an idealized image of ourselves. Of course, in a pluralistic society we acknowledge the desirability of variety, but the amount of variety we are willing to promote is always limited and the basic guide to our curriculum decisions is our calculation of what will most likely make children in our image. And, indeed, why not? What else do we have to go by? It is just important to be clear about it, important for understanding how best to deal with curriculum issues.

CONCLUSION

It would be possible without much difficulty to identify a variety of other presuppositions. Indeed, it should be possible to chart a fairly exhaustive set, though the few outlined above suggest that such a set would require organizing in a hierarchy of levels of generalization. No doubt some of those dealt with could be, at least partially, collapsed together or better formulated in different ways. For example,

Center of value: society/individual might provide a better way of organizing some of the issues touched on above. *Truth: relative/ objective* might lead to a more profound way of categorizing some of the content issues. But we will leave this task of elaboration for elsewhere, and consider the implications of these presuppositions for curriculum arguments and decisions.

If we argue about whether the store on the corner sells paint, and your ground for opposing my claim is your belief that there is no store on the corner, how should we resolve our conflict? It is not an issue that is likely to be resolved by protracted debate, though such a debate might persuade one of us that he had confused corners; it just might resolve the issue by providing greater clarity about it. If I agree that if there is no store on the corner then I will acknowledge my claim is false, then the resolution of this argument is a straightforward empirical matter. We got to the corner to see if there is a store there. If there is not, you win. If there is, we go in to see whether it sells paint.

If I argue on behalf of open education, and your basic grounds for opposing my claims, whether you make the grounds explicit or not, are that human nature is generally untrustworthy, that culture is external, how should we resolve our conflict? It is clearly not a straightforward empirical matter. An attempt at an empirical evaluation of the relative merits of an "open" school and a traditional school might well indicate that on social or humanistic measures—student freedom, happiness, comfort, feelings about teachers and fellow students, and so forth — the "open" school scores higher, and that on measures of academic achievement the "traditional" school scores higher. The obvious problem is that the presuppositions that lead to preferring one kind of school over the other also lead to valuing one kind of measure over the other. That is, both claim victory from the comparison. (In such a general comparison the traditional school is more vulnerable. The "open" school will tend to value its procedures above any product, and thus, as long as it practices openness in its procedures there is no way to undermine its confidence; if the "open" school should show superior academic achievement, the rationale for the traditionalist is entirely undermined.) Our point here is simply that no general empirical test can resolve our dispute because our general objectives differ no less than our procedures.

Is the best procedure then to expose our *presuppositions* to an empirical test? How does one run an experiment to determine whether human nature is generally good or bad? Proponents of the "bad" human nature position tend to argue that history is the experiment and the results are conclusive. But then the proponents of the "good" human nature position tend to argue that history only proves that institutions dehumanize people and prevent their natural goodness from finding an outlet. To the former, history is a charnel house of slaughter and cruelty, with moments of relief; to the latter it is the story of the human spirit's increasingly successful struggle for freedom.

But this is not to say that argument about even so general a presupposition must be ineffective. Examples and reasons strongly articulated in debate may occasionally be effective in causing someone to reassess a position on, say, the likelihood that increasing student choice will lead to improvements in learning. Also, such debate might lead to agreement on some objective held in common by the proponents of "open" and traditional education and in turn that agreement might lead to an empirical test of which procedure was better able to bring about the common objective. For example, it might be agreed by both parties that mastery of basic reading and writing skills is so important an objective that, within limits, each side is willing to sacrifice some degree of either their rigor or openness for the better achievement of that end. An empirical test could be conducted to discover which procedure was generally more fruitful in achieving mastery of the specified skills. Our point here is simply that it is possible to open up to empirical testing areas of dispute based on differing suppositions—however restricted the likely result.

It seems to have become generally accepted that curriculum problems are "practical, not theoretic ones."[7] An implication of what was said just before is that this claim is false. Curriculum problems are theoretical, empirical, and practical. In this they are like the problems of that other common human activity—politics. Underlying political arguments and decisions are presuppositions not unlike some of those I have sketched above. The realm of practical maneuver in politics is perhaps a little greater than in curriculum. Achieving practical results, like winning votes, is sought by various means of persuasion, and exuding of charisma. Similarly, proponents of a particular curriculum position use various, usually more consciously rational, means of persuasion, and charisma is replaced by a kind of authority — the authority and confidence the well-educated person carries in discussions about education. The area for empirical inquiry is somewhat larger in curriculum than politics. But in both, to differing degrees, the problems have a theoretical dimension that may lead to empirical inquiries, in turn leading to practical decisions or results.

If the basic grounds of disagreements about curriculum issues are differing presuppositions, then are we not reduced to complete relativism? Even though it may be that theoretical discussion and empirical inquiry and practical action may occasionally affect some change in someone's presuppositions, does it not simply boil down to a position where everyone is as right as everyone else—where there are no grounds for saying one area of the continuum of a presupposition is better or worse than any other? No: only people who require impossible absolutes and certainties will conclude that the impossibility of achieving them leaves us only with the alternative of absolute relativism. The range open to empirical testing and secure theoretical analysis about practical curriculum concerns may be quite small but that does not mean it does not exist. It does, and it is important to focus a lot of our energy on enlarging it.

This analysis does not lead to relativism for the very good reason that the fact we cannot show which presupposition about, say, human nature is right or wrong does not at all mean that, therefore, all positions are equally right or wrong. Some presuppositions may turn out to be right and others wrong.

That ultimately these presuppositions are like general value positions means that much argument about curriculum problems is likely to be idle *unless* the disputants recognize not just the surface content of their argument but also the basic differences in presuppositions from which their disagreement springs. Making these explicit and trying to isolate components that can be opened to empirical testing or rigorous analysis will lead to less vacuous idleness in our theoretical discussions and lead toward greater rationality in both argument and decision-making. The fact that our basic values and presuppositions are greatly resistant to change does not mean that they do not or cannot change, or that we cannot change other people's. If curriculum is a kind of political venture whose purpose is to create a system that will tend to produce people like ourselves, let us be as sensible as possible in promoting such a system.

What other implications follow from this brief analysis? One seems to be that when we think about curriculum problems and imagine that we are dealing with the particular problem on its merits, our view of its merits is *determined* by the presuppositions with which we approach it. That is, it is an illusion to consider our everyday thinking about curriculum problems to be free. We are not so much thinking, as letting our presuppositions think themselves out. Our thinking is better described as sorting the elements of the new problem into the categories prepared by our presuppositions. This metaphor overstates the case, of course. It suggests absolute rigidity at the level of presupposition and absolute fluidity at the level of content. In fact, the content of curriculum can also, though more rarely and less profoundly, cause changes in the categories created by our presuppositions. We can think about the categories our presuppositions create and we can examine our presuppositions. They are not easy to think *about* because they are the things we think *with*, but there is a sense in which we also think with the phenomena of the world; it is by being sensitive to the world that we can create some slight reference system for our presuppositions.

It is disfunctional, then, to argue about or even think about curriculum problems while failing to recognize the source of our beliefs, arguments, and feelings. Ignorance of our presuppositions and ignorance that our thinking is largely determined by these presuppositions blinds us to the real nature of our disagreements about curriculum decisions. It leads us to believe that our opponents are wicked charlatans and idiots because they reach different conclusions based on the same premises. Recognition of our differing presuppositions, however, would show that our premises are in fact different. It would also allow us to focus much more precisely on those areas where we might work toward resolving disagreements and help us to be more tolerant of persisting disagreements.

Many of these implications are true for decision-making about the socializing curriculum. In that curriculum the realm that can be opened to empirical testing and rigorous analysis seems greater because of the tangible reality of the society that serves as a referent. For the educational curriculum, these implications are more acutely relevant because competing educational theories will usually rest on conflicting presuppositions.

CHAPTER EIGHT

Teaching, Instructing, and Their Different Objectives

A CRUCIAL DIFFERENCE between socializing and educating becomes apparent when we try to state our aims for our socializing curriculum and for our educational curriculum. It is more difficult to make educational aims sound as precise as socializing aims. Again, the socializing curriculum has a more or less determinate objective: to equip students with the knowledge, skills, and attitudes necessary for them to become effective agents within a particular society. The aims of a socializing curriculum in the Soviet Union and in the United States would be rather different, but they would share a degree of clarity about what knowledge, skills, and attitudes they should be inculcating.

To return to the distinction sketched in chapter one, the socializing curriculum might well include as an aim that students learn about the history of their nation and community, whereas the educational curriculum may have as an aim "the development of an historical consciousness." This educational aim does not readily direct us to any particular content. We can't study everything so how do make the choices that will enable us best to achieve our educational aim?

The general socializing aim seems more easily transformed into more particular objectives than does the educational aim. One energetic movement is arguing that effectiveness in schooling will only follow if we convert our general aims into particular objectives and use these objectives as the determiners of our lesson and unit plans. Insofar as this movement gains ground in influencing educational practice, it will likely support the growth of the socializing curriculum, with its apparent relative vagueness. We argue that this move may be appropriate for the socializing curriculum, but is not appropriate for the educational curriculum. In order to make this argument, we look at some aspects of the research aimed at generating a theory of instruction.

Why is research on teaching effectiveness expected to contribute toward a theory of instruction? Why not toward a theory of teaching? The two words are, of course, used quite casually and often interchangeably, but the common preference in this research for the word *instruction* is indicative of a hint of a sense of a distinction between instructing and teaching. It may be suspected by some that *instructing* is a more precise or value-neutral term than *teaching*, that *instructing* has become yet more precise in the fairly technical meaning it has accumulated operationally in the program of research aimed at generating a theory of instruction. But it is not more precise: it just refers to simpler phenomena than does *teaching*. We attempt to draw a sensible distinction between the two terms and the distinct phenomena they refer to. Given the meaning *instruction* has accumulated, we suggest that this term is appropriate when applied to socializing activities but that the significant differences between socializing and educating justify reserving the term *teaching* for educational activities.

TEACHING AND INSTRUCTIONAL THEORY

Some teaching is better than other teaching. Some teachers are better than others. In what ways? The aim of research on teaching effectiveness is to answer this question, and in answering it, to generate a theory of instruction. Initially, such a program of research may seek simple correlations between particular teaching behaviors and learning outcomes. Even casual observation allows us to see things in individual teachers' practice that seem to enhance or inhibit individual students' learning; so, it is expected that bringing "scientific method" to bear on this relationship should reveal more precise and generalizable principles of good teaching. Unfortunately for the hope of easy success, casual observation also shows that a characteristic we might identify as a cause of one teacher's success may seem in the case of another teacher to be irrelevant to the quality of teaching or even a cause of poor teaching. Mr. Smith's flare for the dramatic might be electrifying, whereas Mr. Jones's flare for the dramatic might make one want to throw up.

Usually reviews of the considerable body of research on this topic tell us nothing unambiguously; the findings are either insignificant or inconsistent.[1] The consistent failure of this program of research to yield secure generalizations has encouraged some of its proponents to be more modest in their expectations, at least in the short term. But even so, it seems clear to scientific psychologists that the "folk-wisdom" and commonsense principles that serve imprecisely in the training of teachers should be replaced by at least "concepts, or variables, and their interrelations in the form of weak laws, generalizations, or trends."[2] N.L. Gage, for example, in accepting that there are good reasons to expect that small-scale experiments will continue to yield insignificant or conflicting results, suggests that many of such results will agglomerate into groupings of findings that are regular and consistent. (Even so, he feels it necessary to defend his optimism.)[3]

On the face of it, research aimed at producing even weak laws or generalizations about effective teaching encounters formidable difficulties. The conditions in which scientific methods have worked well seem to be largely absent: one cannot reliably presuppose consistency in teacher and student behaviors, in their understandings and feelings about various subjects and topics, in their shifting distractions, in their changing environments, *ad, vero, infinitum*; one cannot easily see what might count as a unit of teaching or instructing, or a unit of education, or a unit of learning that can be isolated for study. That is, there is the danger that in selecting units in this research, these units will not be units of the phenomenon one set out to study. Again, from casual observation, what should count as evidence of effective teaching is problematic. The profoundest effects may not show for a week or a year. Indeed, the most important effects may not be evident until after the particulars through which they have wrought their work are forgotten, or the particulars may flit virtually unhindered through the students' awareness but yet may serve in their passage to restructure some general scheme that profoundly determines their thinking or their way of making sense of things.

The researcher might want to discount such things on the reasonable grounds that one should start by securing knowledge about more straightforward aspects of human teaching and learning. The problem is that there are no more straightforward aspects. These kinds of complexities are central features of teaching and learning in education. Discounting or ignoring any aspect of the phenomena in favor of what one's methodology can handle may be methodologically permissible as long as one does not forget what one has discounted or ignored.

What is a theory of instruction supposed to look like? A fairly generally accepted image was set out by Jerome S. Bruner some years ago.[4] Such a theory of instruction should specify how best to predispose children favorably toward learning; should specify how materials should be organized or structured to make them optimally graspable by students; should specify the most effective sequences in which to present the materials; and should specify the nature and pacing of rewards and punishments in the process of learning and teaching. Such a theory must be prescriptive, setting forth rules concerning the most effective ways of teaching and learning. It must be normative, setting forth criteria and stating the conditions for meeting them. Such a prescriptive and normative theory of instruction, in addition, "must be congruent with these [descriptive] theories of learning and development to which it subscribes."[5]

There seem to be grounds to question what Bruner might mean by the theory of instruction being "congruent" with the descriptive theories of learning and development, and to question in what sense it is to "subscribe" to them. He certainly does not seem to mean only that the prescriptive theory will not contravene what they describe is the case. Does he mean, for example, that the end-point described by the theory of development provides objectives and criteria for the instructional theory's prescriptions?[6] And what implications for the theory of instruction follow from the insecurity of currently available learning theories?[7]

To begin with, then, the commonly accepted image of what a theory of instruction should look like seems to require psychological theories of a kind we now lack. Clearly, if one accepts the presuppositions on which the program of scientific psychology rests, one does not sit around waiting for adequate theories of development and learning before trying to articulate one's theory of instruction. One goes ahead in the reasonable hope that there will be a dialectical development whereby work on the theory of instruction may contribute toward refinement of the theories of learning and development. Those presuppositions will also encourage the researcher to disregard or depreciate any apparent distinction between instructing in particulars and teaching. Instructing will be seen as a straightforward constituent of education—an educational theory may well prescribe *what* should be learned in order to attain a particular ideal of educational experience, and the theory of instruction may be put to work to ensure the efficient learning of whatever content is required as a constituent of that ideal.

APTITUDE-TREATMENT INTERACTIONS

Let us look briefly at the research aimed at discovering empirical generalizations about the relationship between teaching behaviors and learning outcomes and see what this seems to offer toward the kind of theory of instruction Bruner proposes. The course of a central part of this research has been well described in Lee J. Cronbach's two "two disciplines" papers.[8]

In the first of these papers, Cronbach charted the failure of scientific psychology to come to grips adequately with the problems involved in generating a theory of instruction. He recommended as a move toward a solution to those problems that experimental psychology should join forces with correlational psychology, marrying the rigorous treatments of the former to the latter's greater sophistication in dealing with individual differences. So instead of continuing to seek fruitlessly for the best method of teaching everyone—finding the best instructional "treatment"—psychologists should try to discover what treatments best suit different people's different "aptitudes." Aptitudes, Cronbach pointed out, clearly interact differently with different treatments. Thus, for example, an aggressive extrovert might learn more easily from group discussion than a shy introvert might; the latter might more easily than the former learn from private study. Scientific research, then, might tell us what kinds of people learn best by what kinds of methods. Thus, instead of using a particular method of teaching that suits only a proportion of a group of students—and interacts effectively with only a proportion of aptitudes—we might train teachers to use, or make available, say, three or four "treatments" suited to a much wider range of aptitutdes. In an ideal world each student would receive the treatment best suited to his or her aptitudes. The finding and securing of such "Aptitude-Treatment Interactions" (ATIs) "will carry us into an educational psychology which measures readiness for different types of teaching and which invents teaching methods to fit different types of readiness."[9]

An initial objection to this program, more clear with hindsight, might be to note that no one "has" *an* aptitude; rather each person also "has" an intelligence, a set of personal relationships with teachers and other students, varying distractions and fluctuating abilities to control them, desires, hopes, and the usual changing array of complicated things we imprecisely distinguish and crudely name.

Nearly twenty years later, Cronbach reported on the considerable body of research on ATIs. In describing the attempts he made, with

Richard Snow, at synthesizing the research reports, he notes: "In attempting to generalize from the literature, Snow and I have been thwarted by the inconsistent findings coming from roughly similar inquiries."[10] And while some ATIs seem somewhat generalizable, one cannot make any secure generalizations because other ATIs seem to interfere with them. Other personality factors, experiences, environments, and so on, prevent one from concluding anything very securely about how best to teach anyone. "However far we carry our analysis — to third order or fifth order or any other — untested interactions of a still higher order can be envisioned."[11]

Cronbach's conclusion is rather pessimistic for the program set forth some twenty years earlier:

> Our troubles do not arise because human events are in principle unlawful; man and his creations are part of the natural world. The trouble, as I see it, is that we cannot store up enough generalizations and constructs for ultimate assembly into a network. It is as if we needed a gross of dry cells to power an engine and could only make one a month. The energy would leak out of the first cells before we had half the battery completed. So it is with the potency of our generalizations.[12]

One problem with the program, Cronbach states, is that "too narrow an identification with science, however, has fixed our eyes on an inappropriate goal."[13] Instead of seeking secure generalizations and aiming toward a general theory, however, it may be considered reasonable to develop small-scale, locally applicable ATIs that will help teachers in particular schools teach particular things to particular students — thereby using the power amassed in one of the dry cells rather than letting it leak away while trying to amass enough to power an engine.

Let us consider Snow's proposal for developing local theories. He begins with the same general observation as Cronbach: "As work on aptitude-treatment interactions (ATIs) has proceeded, it has become clear that interactions, both among individual difference variables and between them and instructional conditions, can be so complex as to push generalizations beyond our grasp, practically speaking."[14] (If our concern is practicality, one may reasonably wonder about the practicality of the kind of large-scale research effort necessary to generate even small-scale ATIs — especially when one recalls that Cronbach and Snow's analysis of the ATI research involved rejecting the greater part of it as so flawed as to be useless.) Snow concludes that while we cannot hope to generate a general theory of instruction we might hope to generate local theories of instruction. "ATI does not make theory impossible; it makes general theory impossible."[15]

A strong argument for not following the path recommended in Snow's proposal has already been made. Roger Gehlbach points out that a crucial reason why the search for more general ATIs and a general theory of instruction has foundered remains to undermine the more modest proposal:

> A major commitment to local theories would be premature . . . [because] it presumes *enough* of the *right kinds* of instructional hypotheses have been subjected to appropriate research designs to justify a massive restructuring of the goals for instructional research. . . . A merely realigned focus of attention to local theory construction is not going to solve many problems if the conceptual clarity, methodological rigor and analytic quality of educational research do not improve generally. If, on the other hand, the overall quality of research does improve, then local theories may be unnecessary in our search for generalizable findings.[16]

A purpose in seeking general theories was the establishment of laws; that is, one could explain one's phenomena, and so one could intervene in them confident that one could predict the results caused by particular interventions. What one loses with the reduced ambition to generate only local theories is confidence in explaining causal sequences and consequently confidence that a future intervention will produce results similar to those of a past intervention.

Gehlbach further points out that the discovery of ATIs may not be best met with the assumption that one must in instruction "accommodate" to them. Rather, Gehlbach argues, it might be better "to find ways to *eliminate* them (e.g., by developing more powerful instructional methods)."[17] So, if we develop more powerful instructional methods that are effective across the range of normal aptitude differentials, ATI research may become simply a diagnostic tool for detecting weak instructional strategies.

From where, however, are we going to develop more powerful instructional methods? These were supposed to be the promised product of a theory of instruction, which was to have been built with help from ATI research. If ATI research does establish some generalizable ATI findings, how will our theory of instruction know which should be accommodated to and which eliminated? Gehlbach's suggested aim of eliminating ATIs seems to return us to the program criticized as fruitless in the first of Cronbach's "two disciplines" papers. If we *can* generate more powerful instructional strategies from some source other than a theory of instruction — say from folk-wisdom — we might ask why we need a theory of instruction. Presumably to systematize and generalize, from empirical study, these products of folk-wisdom. But this is what the program of research has failed to do, and is what Cronbach and Snow have concluded it cannot do — except in local circumstances. And this local program Gehlbach has given us reasons to believe is quite impracticable.

Another way of looking at the oddity of the ATI research program is to consider that the more successful it is, the more difficult it becomes to achieve its goals — both the goal of generating a general theory of instruction and the connected goal of practical pay-off. If people had two or three distinguishable aptitudes then matters might be relatively straightforward. Discovering by experiment the two or three treatments that interact optimally with these aptitudes would provide some practical guidance to the instructor. But if we find twenty distinguishable aptitudes, for each of which we have discovered the optimal treatment, what do we do? We are faced with insurmountable problems. Aptitude A, let us say, interacts optimally with treatment A^1. That is, if instructed by method A^1 the person with aptitude A will learn better. But learn better than what? Well, learn better than if instructed with treatment B^1. The usual form of ATI research is to pose what seem like binary opposite aptitudes (high/low anxiety, serialist/wholist, etc.) and find treatments that best suit the distinct poles. So if we have twenty such clearly established ATIs, how are we to discover whether a person with aptitude A is indeed best instructed by treatment A^1? That is, the person with aptitude A may also have fairly high aptitudes D, J, L, R, V, Z. Do we pretest each individual on each aptitude? And could we design treatments to suit the infinite variety of mixed aptitudes? Perhaps an example might be useful here.

Let us take an ATI more or less at random. If our aim is to improve the effectiveness of our instructional efficiency, G. Pask and B. C. E. Scott's research[18] suggests we should divide our students into two groups, the one made up of those students who seem to learn better from what Pask and Scott call a "serialist" treatment, and the other made up from those who seem to learn better from a "wholist" treatment. Among the ATIs reported this seems a fairly dramatic, unsuspected, and successful case. The serialist and wholist strategies seem to offer a contribution toward our armamentarium of instructional devices.

In what way does this knowledge contribute toward articulation of a theory of instruction? If we are aiming at a general theory presumably this finding would play a part. Crudely, one might incorporate it as a rule that after pretesting and distinguishing serialists from wholists one should use the appropriate treatment for the appropriate group. This rule, however, would have to be incorporated with a rule recommending different treatments for, say, extroverts and introverts, for high I.Q. and low I.Q., for high creativity and low creativity, for high I.Q./low creativity and low I.Q./high creativity, and so on. That is, if the program were successful in discovering twenty clear, generalizable ATIs, they would leave us with a theory of instruction too cumbersome to use. Even if we are satisfied that we will settle for local findings, how do we decide which of the available ATIs we should use? Presumably Pask and Scott's finding applies vividly to the experimental group, and if we wish to instruct them, then that ATI is useful. Treating one group in a serialist way and the other in a wholist way ensures that both groups will learn more than if a neutral treatment is used. But what, in this complex world, is a neutral treatment? Perhaps that particular group divided even more dramatically between high and low anxiety, and if they were divided into high and low anxiety groups and the appropriate treatments were used perhaps the learning of the whole group might have been dramatically superior to that achieved by the serialist/wholist division.

These are problems raised for instruction. When our concern turns to teaching, and thus education, we have additional problems if our hope is to use the results of ATI research for practical improvements. To continue with the particular example above: we have to wonder what is serialism and what is wholism. Are they descriptive of brain differences? Or do they result from different kinds of teaching? Are they independent of I.Q., creativity, anxiety level, and so forth? Are they skills that everyone has but uses differentially for different tasks? Are they ends of a continuum or points on some more extensive continuum?

If our concern is simple instruction, then we may be able to use this finding in particular cases. But if our concern is teaching, to accept straightforwardly that serialists should be taught serially and wholists wholistically is to commit the psychological fallacy. A description of something that is not a constraint of nature does not imply any educational prescription. Perhaps the teacher should follow Gehlbach's recommendation and find an instructional strategy that will eliminate the ATI—that will teach serialists and wholists equally well, achieving for all students acceptable minimum performance.

Perhaps the teacher should teach serialists in a wholistic way and wholists in a serial way, in order to develop greater flexibility in the thinking of the two groups. In such a case, of course, the teaching of the particular content would be subordinate to teaching greater flexibility of thinking. Perhaps serialism is an inferior form of thinking and should be extirpated, and serialists should be taught to become wholists.

INSTRUCTIONAL OBJECTIVES

Elaborations of Bruner's model for a theory of instruction usually include the requirement that a part of any instructional strategy must involve the specification of instructional objectives. Let us briefly look at this area to see what contribution it makes toward a theory of instruction and what implications it might have for education.

It is commonly assumed by researchers in the tradition of scientific psychology that education's folk-wisdom principle that it is usually useful for the teacher to sketch out the aims of any particular unit in advance and it is usually useful to let students know in advance what is to be learned, can be turned, by the use of a "scientific method," into a precise principle that can enormously improve instructional efficiency. There has been a huge body of writing about such precise principles under the heading of "behavioral objectives" or "criterion-referenced instruction." (This rather tortured term suggests, in one of its common interpretations, that the objective to modify students' behavior in a particular way serves as the criterion which is used to judge the appropriateness of all parts of the instructional act.) These are key tools in developing instructional strategies that will control students' behavior in the direction of more efficient learning:

> It is clear that a model or theory of instruction is in fact a special case of what has come to be known in the mathematical and engineering literature as *optimal control theory*, or, more simply, control theory. The development of control theory has progressed at a rapid rate both in the United States and abroad, but most of the applications involve engineering or economic systems of one type or another. Precisely the same problems are posed in the area of instruction except that the system to be controlled is the human learner, rather than a machine or group of industries.[19]

When Richard Atkinson notes that precisely the same problems are posed, we must agree that one can pose the problem about controlling human learning in a form that is exactly analogous to the way the problem of the control of an engineering function may be posed. Whether posing it this way will enable one to answer it adequately is another question. In order to study this question it is necessary to be precise about what effective instruction is being effective at, and so it needs to be known precisely how we can tell whether or not any particular instructional act has been effective. Thus, it seems to follow, for any instructional unit, objectives need to be spelled out in precise terms, and there needs to be some means of measuring precisely whether or not those objectives have been achieved. So a statement of objectives needs to be a mirror image of what is to be evaluated at the end of the instructional act. What is to be evaluated must then be measurable in terms of some observable behavioral change, and so the objectives need to be stated in terms of the behavioral changes that the instructional act will bring about.

Now a point in passing: these procedures are designed in order to study instruction, to find out what kind of instructional strategies work in which kinds of circumstances with what kinds of people. Note the unthinking ease with which experimental procedures are converted directly into recommended procedures for practice within education. Conditions made necessary in order *to study* instruction are asserted to be the best for *the practice* of teaching, even before the study has yielded any clear results. This observation seems either to be not noted or not thought at all odd by proponents of the use of behavioral objectives.

Much of the contention about behavioral objectives in education has turned on some teachers' claims that their aim is, say, to teach "an appreciation of the beauty of Shakespeare's sonnets," or to teach toward "the development of an historical consciousness." These teachers claim that these things cannot be expressed in behavioral terms. Proponents of the use of behavioral objectives tend to respond that while indeed such a general aim must remain ineffable in some sense, constituents of this general aim are not. That is, the teachers who claim to have these general aims nevertheless have to do something on Monday morning and that "something" will be a constituent of the general aim; and if the teachers can express what is to be taught on Monday morning and how they will recognize whether or not it has been learned, then the technology of behavioral objectives may help in making the learning of this constituent of the general aim more effective. So from general educational aims may be derived particular instructional objectives. The achievement of these objectives is the job that criterion-referenced instruction can make clear and efficient, and in the accumulation of such achieved objectives the educational aim may be also achieved (insofar as it can be stated in terms that allow one to perceive whether or not it has been achieved).

Within the writings about behavioral objectives a fairly simple distinction tends to be accepted: "aims" are vague and long-term; "objectives" are precise and relatively short-term, and their achievement can be precisely measured if they are properly stated. There are, though, some distinctions made among objectives — for example, "expressive," "experiential," and so on.[20] Also, it is assumed that objectives may be fairly straightforwardly "derived" from aims. Both the distinction between "aims" and "objectives," and the assumption about deriving one from the other involve problems that are largely ignored in these writings,[21] but they will be passed over here, at least as they are posed in those terms, as they are peripheral to the argument.[22]

Only two points about behavioral objectives in education are relevant to the present argument: the first is a simple empirical matter; the second helps to crystalize why many good teachers (and no doubt bad ones) and many sensible educators (and no doubt senseless ones) oppose them.

Proponents of behavioral objectives adopt in their writings the authority of science. They treat opponents as might the medical scientist carrying to witless diseased peasants a cure which they resist on grounds of primitive superstition. Now the excessive self-confidence with which proponents of behavioral objectives or criterion-referenced instruction insist that their technology will improve educational practice is such that one assumes their prescriptions must have the backing of overwhelming empirical support. On no other grounds could they so confidently turn their experimental procedures into educational prescriptions. This program involves a simple empirical claim: instruction (and teaching) that uses behavioral objectives in the prescribed form will be more effective than instruction (and teaching) that doesn't, other things being equal. (The final phrase, of course, provides reasons for expecting some ambiguity in any results from comparative experiments.) Such an empirical claim is embedded in assertions such as: "The more explicit the instructor can be regarding the statement of instructional objectives, the better. The only kind of specificity that really helps in improving teacher behavior empirically is the specification of goals in terms of student behavior changes."[23] Or: "A statement of an objective is useful to the extent that it specifies what the learner must be able to *do* or perform when he is demonstrating his mastery of the objective."[24]

Proponents of such a program are not claiming that it will merely make instruction a little more efficient: "In our view this development is one of the most important educational advances of the 1900s and signals a very significant attack upon the problems of education."[25] The somewhat bizarre feature of all this is that there is scant empirical support that even the simplest and crudest instructional tasks are improved in efficacy by the use of these procedures.[26] There is virtually no convincing support, that is, for these strong claims when applied to instruction, and their easy application to education — which we have yet to come to—is a scientistic romantic fantasy.

The second point we want to make is that one cannot put a unit of education into the form of a behavioral objective. It is assumed without question in the writings of proponents of these procedures that while vague aims like "appreciating the beauty of Shakespeare's sonnets" or "developing an historical consciousness" cannot be put into behavioral terms, constituents of these can be put into the form of precise objectives. A simple preliminary point: "appreciating the beauty of Shakespeare's sonnets" or "developing an historical consciousness" are no more *vague* than the most rigorous behavioral objective. They are precise referents to complex phenomena. "Appreciating the beauty of Shakespeare's sonnets" refers to an experience, a rather refined one based on a range of knowledge and experiences, and one which will be in some ways different for different people. None of this makes it imprecise or "ineffable." It may make it immeasurable by the gauges educational psychologists have available, or know how to "read," but this is quite another thing from the aim's being imprecise. We cannot measure the pain of a toothache, but that hardly makes one's toothache vague and imprecise. If we dismiss what we cannot measure precisely we have no incentive to increase the sophistication of our measuring tools.

The point is that if one wants to break up an educational aim into constituent units one has to be sure that the units are indeed units of the thing one is aiming to compose from them. It is taken for granted by proponents of educational objectives that educational units are fairly straightforward. Teachers teach History by means of facts and concepts. If one opens a history book, therefore, one has on the page constituent units of education. If a teacher wants to object and say no, these bits and pieces are only the means to help students "develop an historical consciousness," the educational psychologist writes off this "vague" general aim as irrelevant to the area where the technology of behavioral objectives may help make the teaching task more efficient.

A metaphor may help here. The technology of behavioral objectives works by dividing a teaching topic into units. It is assumed that in doing this the instructional technologist is doing nothing different from what the teacher does in breaking down a topic into units and lessons, except that the technologist is being more precise and efficient. There is, however, a crucial difference. Let us consider the general educational aim as an image or picture. The instructional technologist assumes that the picture can be broken into constituent bits and pieces, and when these bits and pieces are put together one has reconstituted the picture. If, that is, the general educational aim can be stated precisely enough, it can be broken into constituent objectives. Then the student may use the recommended procedures to learn efficiently, thereby achieving the general educational aim. Our point is that this notion is false because in education the images or pictures of our general aims are not of a kind amenable to this treatment: there are no such two-dimensional pictures; to continue the metaphor, educational aims instead are like holograms.

If the photographic plate containing the interference pattern of the holographic image is broken into bits and pieces, each piece contains, in however blurred a form, the image of the whole. The ear of the Mona Lisa tells nothing of the lady's smile. A small section of the holographic image of a modern enigmatic lady would, with the laser's light, reveal, however vaguely, the bewitching smile and ear and chin and all the rest. An educational objective should be seen as more like a piece of a hologram than a piece of a two-dimensional picture. This suggests why one cannot specify an *educational* objective, or teaching objective in education, in behavioral terms unless one can also specify the general educational aim in behavioral terms; one cannot specify behavioral objectives for a lesson on the causes of the French Revolution unless one can also specify in behavioral terms what it means to possess an historical consciousness. There are no instructional constituents which do not entail the image of the whole.

Now this may appear a bit arcane. Is it to be denied that instructing students efficiently about the main facts, concepts, and causes of the French Revolution is of no educational value? Everyone surely recognizes a sense in which such knowledge may be worthless, may remain inert for some people, but may be used in educational development, may provide an aliment for others. Whitehead's observation that the merely well-informed man is the greatest bore on God's earth catches the sense in which education requires something in addition to facts, concepts, and causes. What is it that in some cases makes a set of facts and concepts of no educational value and in others makes the same facts and concepts of the greatest value? What is it that in some cases makes a set of facts and concepts not educational units? Our metaphor is intended to point toward the answer that what makes a set of facts and concepts educational units is that they contain in their organization an image of the whole of which they are units. What makes the same set of facts and concepts educationally inert in some cases is that they are not units of an educational whole. The technology of behavioral objectives guarantees that its units will be of the latter kind, educationally inert.

Still arcane, perhaps. The proponents of behavioral objectives may respond that all they are recommending is that we do efficiently something that is normally done inefficiently. While teaching is no doubt often done inefficiently, the proponents of behavioral objectives offer a plan that is even less efficient than poor teaching if their goal is an educational one. But if learning about the French Revolution serves an educational aim, how can instructing students in the main facts and concepts about the French Revolution not contribute toward that aim? Surely knowing such facts and concepts is a necessary condition for understanding or appreciating the French Revolution. So even if we insist that knowing such facts and concepts is not a *sufficient* condition for understanding the French Revolution, why cannot the technology of behavioral objectives be used in teaching the *necessary* knowledge and do whatever else is necessary to make understanding possible? Because this procedure presupposes a distinction that does not exist in education. In education there is no such thing as an objective, a piece, that does not entail at the same time the general aim. The general aim to develop an historical consciousness and, as a part of that, to teach an understanding of the French Revolution and, as a part of that, to teach the ten main facts, seven main concepts, and four main causes of the French Revolution, yields a situation where one cannot properly teach the ten main facts, seven main concepts, and four main causes of the French Revolution without at the same time teaching the development of an historical consciousness. That one can instruct in the facts, concepts, and causes independently of the general aim is obviously the case—and one can use behavioral objectives in the process—but the case is no longer an educational one. The particulars in such a case are not like parts of a hologram—the laser's light leaves us only with an ear or a bit of hair. The more general image has to be ever-present in each particular to make it an educational aliment.

The second point, then, is that the kind of unit one can put into the form of an instructional objective cannot be an educational unit.

Certainly one can assert that these behavioral objectives, when achieved, accumulate into a picture which may indeed look like one of education's holograms—or, at least, they may look like holograms if one persuades the looker to stand dead still and close one eye. And no doubt in the land of the blind such one-eyed observers will seem like kings. If we open both eyes and move about, however, the difference between a hologram and a two-dimensional picture is vivid and fundamental. The sense of strain in making this distinction with regard to the reality of educational phenomena is that it is so obvious that everyone recognizes it; but if someone suddenly insists on standing dead still with one eye closed, it is not easy to point out how the image of the picture is fundamentally different from that of the hologram. If one claims that words like "appreciate" and "understand" cannot be used then it is indeed rather difficult to point out the difference between being able to repeat a set of inert facts and concepts and being able to understand and appreciate what those facts and concepts refer to. The point is that there is no reason at all to forbid use of the words: they are perfectly clear; they refer to things we all recognize; they serve to help us make crucial distinctions between clearly distinguishable things; and they are frequently extremely precise referents to complex phenomena that exist and cannot be adequately referred to by using any other terms. This is to say that the linguistic constraints insisted on by proponents of behavioral objectives are entirely arbitrary and serve—like standing dead still with one eye closed—only to block out from one's range of vision absolutely crucial aspects of the phenomena one is supposed to be looking at and studying. Ignoring parts of one's phenomena of interest is not rational, so it can hardly be properly recommended as scientific.

But what is it that makes some facts and concepts educational units? And if that can be answered precisely, do we not provide things on which the technology of behavioral objectives may work? And surely all those teachers who have been forced by their school boards to write their objectives in behavioral terms are not thereby made into mere instructional technologists unable to contribute to their students' education. First, and fortunately, the complexity of practice will ensure that teachers will not merely instruct toward the achievement of their stated behavioral objectives; they will also teach by imbuing the particulars with more general and diffuse aims. Indeed, in most cases the writing of behavioral objectives will have very little influence on actual teaching—a fact already noted and bewailed by their proponents.

An oddity of educational, as distinct from instructional, objectives is that their achievement in each individual case may be different. The sophisticated historical consciousness of A. J. P. Taylor is quite different from that of G. R. Elton, which in turn is different from that of F. Braudel, and so on. Similarly, each individual child will develop an historical consciousness—where it is achieved at all—by different means, using different facts and concepts in different combinations. Yet "historical consciousness" is the precise term to use for the educational objective toward which the good teacher steers each child. It is the criterion by which one tries to decide in each individual case whether a particular form of knowledge is an educational unit or not.

CONCLUSION

Education, like love and pain, is an experience. Like love and pain it is crystal clear at times and yet not amenable to precise formulation in words. One might wisely suspect a love that could be confined in words. Like love and pain, education is ultimately a personal experience whose nature is a part of the person experiencing, and which ultimately is inaccessible to anyone else. We know something of the causes and processes of love, pain, and education, but we cannot line these up in neat sets of causally connected hierarchies of skills, knowledge, and attitudes. If we see attempts to do this, we may be sure that it is not education they are attempting. Usually we may conclude that it is socializing that they are attempting. Distinguishing one from the other is important, otherwise we may start applying to one of them criteria appropriate only to the other. In the case of stating behavioral objectives, this may be suitable within the socializing curriculum, but to use them within education violates the nature of the phenomenon and its units.

It seems reasonable to generalize this conclusion to the claim that the bulk of what is called educational psychology should be renamed socializational psychology. The methodological presuppositions that prevail within "educational" psychology prevent its engaging matters of educational significance.

CHAPTER NINE

Educational Objectives

IN CHAPTER EIGHT we tried to bring out some differences between instructional units that lend themselves to the technology of behavioral objectives and educational units that are of a more complex and elusive nature than the technology of behavioral objectives can easily accommodate. We have argued that educational objectives are different in kind from behavioral objectives as holograms are different from snapshots. We have emphasized the point that a failure to keep in mind the distinction between education and socialization leads to the mistaken view that *all* of a school's curricula can be reduced to terms that allow their specification in behavioral objectives.

Now we come to the question of how one might go about specifying educational objectives in a way that is more suitable and alimentary to the process of educating. We are not sure that this way of thinking will have any more actual effect on teaching practices than the behavioral objectives way has had on instructional practices. We offer it as a proposal, an alternative that we hope will advance our understanding of the activities of teaching.

We begin with the premise that people who work in public educational institutions, both teachers and students, ought to know more precisely what they are doing. Only in rare circumstances is one better off not knowing what one is doing. For instance one can plead (temporary) insanity under the M'Naghten rule (a man is insane, diseased of mind, when he does not have the "capacity to know the nature and quality of the act — or if he did know it, that he did not know he was doing what was wrong") as a form of defense, for a lighter sentence, for mercy.

Of course, the thought that not only school people but all of us ought to know as precisely as we can what we are doing (especially when it is in the "name" of something—"the preservation of cultural values," "advancement of knowledge," "character development," and the like) is the motivating thought behind many plans for improvements of many kinds. In the case of "specifying behavioral objectives" and "accountability for teachers" this good intention has been schematized into a formal instructional plan. Our point here is that such plans are of dubious worth because 1) it is *impossible* for conscious beings to proceed *entirely without* specified objectives as long as the capacity for intention or even imagination is still operational, and 2) it is clearly undesirable to proceed *entirely within* such a scheme even though it may be theoretically possible to do so. The remedy for these troubles, as we see it, begins in being more specific about the various meanings and component parts of the terms *specify* and *objective*.

We shall leave out the term "behavioral" from the phrase "specifying behavioral objectives" in our analysis for two reasons. First, we have been thoroughly confused about what the term means to those who use it with most confidence—that is, behaviorists—and, therefore, take for ourselves the same caution we urge on them. Here are three sources of our confusion. In *Beyond Freedom and Dignity*, B. F. Skinner suggests that humanists have been wrong in holding individuals to account for what they do because it is "culture" that "induces" the behavior of people, not the other way around. Then he says that culture is a network of relations among people, not merely a collection of them.[1] We are left to conclude that a human being does not, cannot, "induce" behavior, but that several people in "a network of relations" can "induce" behavior. Even if this argument turns out to make sense, we must confess that as of this writing, we don't get it, and we don't understand what "behavior" means in its context. The second source of our confusion is an accomplished behavioral therapist who told us enthusiastically that his grandmother, who liked to bake and give cookies to children, was "really" doing *behavioral modification techniques* essentially no different from the ones he used with his patients. The scope of different circumstances encompassed by this use of the term "behavioral modification" left us to wonder what would be excluded from its reaches. He used the term in a way that suggested a ubiquitous existence of behavioral modification, which for us belittled the concept and dwindled its usefulness. Our last source is a professor of psychology who told us of her current project, an attempt to train persons "to behaviorally modify" their mentalistic urges of such things as affection, depression, joy — she doesn't want to reduce these mentalisms to behaviorisms; she merely wants to use a theory that denies their existence to increase or decrease their occurrences and effects. This inconsistency, added to the first two sources of confusion (no individual can induce behavior, but every grandmother does), is bewildering.

The second reason why we are going to drop the term "behavioral" in this analysis is that it is a superfluous qualifier in the phrase "specifying behavioral objectives." Adequate specification — the description and enumeration of necessary particulars — of an objective will include "actable" or "behavable" evidence for the objective's achievement when such evidence is appropriate and not when not. If one is concerned with the type of objective that calls only for such evidence, it will be so indicated in the specification — the stating of the objective—in terms that can be verified through observation. In the broad sense, anything that can be perceived can be described in behavioral terms even if what we perceive is merely the book *lying* there on the table, *not moving*, or the sun *rising*, or the previously disruptive child now quietly *behaving* himself. In these examples, we don't actually *see* any *behavior* other than nonaction, but we can talk about these observations as if we did. If the term "behavior" does not distinguish between an action and a nonaction in what we perceive, or at least in the way we talk about what we perceive, then we think the term loses its utility and approaches superfluity. Insofar as we are capable of distinguishing this from that (and we must because we cannot perceive everything at once) and recognize that we are doing so, we can specify; insofar as we can intend to act, that is, plan ahead, we can have or make objectives. We obviously do both with ease, all the time. But that's not all we do. We also like surprises.

Each of these terms, *specify* and *objective*, is composed of three aspects that comprise a sort of paradigm for their systematic (as opposed to contingent) use. We can emphasize each of these aspects of *specify* with prefixes: pre-specify, simul-specify, and post-specify. A similar emphasis can be achieved for *objective* with the terms intent, content, and sentiment. Figure 9.1 (p. 124) diagrams the aspects of *specification* and *objectives*.

SPECIFICATION

By the term *specify* we mean to name, describe, and/or enumerate explicitly, in detail. Specification is discrimination, that is, the ability to tell differences. In relation to particular objectives, we must be able first to distinguish one from another objective, and then to decide on adequate criteria for describing them explicitly so that their achievement might be perceptibly detected. We make a serious and

FIGURE 9.1

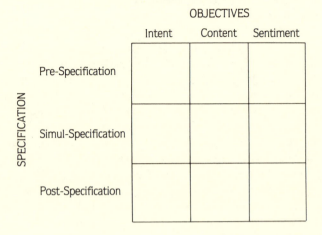

OBJECTIVES

	Intent	Content	Sentiment
Pre-Specification			
Simul-Specification			
Post-Specification			

SPECIFICATION

severely restrictive mistake when we assume that this sort of specification must always be done *before* the objective itself comes into play. We tend to think, for no good reason beyond habit that we know of, that the specifying of an objective must (naturally) take place before one is actually engaged with the objective and certainly before one has finished with it. It is this naive view that stands behind about three-quarters of the controversy over specifying objectives, making such controversy at best unproductive, and, worse, something of an embarrassment to the fields of teaching and evaluation.

There is nothing in the etymology or in the current usages of the term that indicates when such specification should be done. We have every day in North America, for example, courtrooms filled with judges and lawyers and witnesses and juries whose business is the specification of alleged objectives (when there is culpable motive, or negligence when not) that have already been accomplished, or were in the process of being accomplished (as in conspiracy). Specifying after the fact precisely what objectives were met, to what degree, and by whom is an example of a useful, engrossing, active, personalized learning experience. In most cases it is, on several levels, an experience in learning—no matter what else it is. We would even say that learning the skills needed for "telling differences" is itself an educational objective.

The question about specification is, "Under what circumstances is it better or more propitious to pre-specify, simul-specify, or post-specify an objective?" Clearly we *do* all three kinds of specifying but we don't often think of what we do in just these terms. Some examples would help here.

PRE-SPECIFICATION

Of all our colleagues polled on the question, "Do you appreciate the fact that airline pilots must be checked out periodically on an extensive list of pre-specified objectives designed to measure their skills, knowledge, reflexes, and health?" only one expressed indifference (and he is a rather morbid existentialist type who actually prefers "terminal" contracts to tenure). Most of us agree that in this situation it is to our (including the pilot's) advantage that such examining of pre-specified objectives takes place, and that the objectives themselves are best specified beforehand.

Another colleague brings to mind a second example. It is to be preferred, in the majority of cases, that when one undertakes to remodel a portion of one's home, one has plans made — objectives specified—that delineate procedure and outcome, *before* one takes up hammer and saw and sets to.

These are examples justified on socialization criteria. An educational example was suggested earlier; learning the skills of specifying, discriminating, of telling differences is a quality and an objective of being educated.

SIMUL-SPECIFICATION

Sometimes we find ourselves in situations that are confusing in one of two ways — either we confuse another person, or we are confused by other persons or by some nonpersonal elements of the situation. The point is that sometimes we catch ourselves in the act of being at cross purposes with another. The questions, "What are we doing now?" and "Why are we doing this?" are asking those involved to specify what they are doing, what they are up to, what their actual, active purposes are, that is, what objectives are operating. These questions represent the core of small group communication processes, a context whereby a small group of people examine deliberately and thoroughly the objectives, motives, and forms and styles of expression operating in their group *at that time*. In this example, the objective of the group processes is to enlarge the area of shared or "open" information (as opposed to the "hidden-from-other" or the "blind-to-self" information that always exists in some proportion among individuals but not necessarily in a fixed proportion). This is largely done by the sometimes tedious but usually fructuous work of cooperatively helping individuals to discover (literally dis-cover) their partially understood motives and objectives, and the nature of very specific but hitherto unspecified (preconscious?) intentions, needs, desires. In this context, with these purposes, it is most appropriate to work in the present as much as possible, to simul-specify objectives as they surface in transaction. The group leader does this, too, in guiding the progress and idiosyncratic development of the group, toward ends that can be justified either on socialization or on educational criteria.

Another example of the propitious use of simul-specification was suggested to us by something Alan Watts once wrote about travel: "Real travel requires a maximum of unscheduled wandering, for there is no other way of discovering surprises and marvels, which, as I see it, is the only good reason for not staying home."[2] Some people, of course, would rather have a detailed itinerary in the pocket before they lock the back door, but others, like Watts, value the simultaneity, the spontaneous wandering into new objectives, desirable partly because of their unanticipated character.

The difference between this type of specification and the first type mentioned is shown by contrasting the questions "What are you going to do?" and "What are you doing?" The degree of specification or the need for specification is not at issue, only the *timing* of its being done in relation to the objective. The same is true of the last type, post-specification, when the question is "What did you do?"

POST-SPECIFICATION

We have suggested with the courtroom example that the post-specification of objectives is sometimes of great practical value. We would also go on to say that sometimes it is the *only* possible sort of specifying that can be done with regard to some objectives. This claim has some support from social psychology in the form of Festinger's theory of cognitive dissonance, and from psychodynamic theories about the concept of rationalization. We learn from these views that people often act first and think later about what they have done. Reason, or the specification of objectives, is provided after the fact as a way of explaining and justifying particular actions that were performed without an adequate or conscious rationale. Specification follows action with regard to some objectives. The question, "What did you do?" is as educationally interesting as the question "What will you do?" when discussing the specification of objectives.

Freud made much the same point when he wrote:

> But one cannot always carry out one's reasonable intentions. There is often something in the material itself which takes charge of one and diverts one from one's first intentions. Even such a trivial achievement as the arrangement of a familiar piece of material is not entirely subject to an author's own choice; it takes what line it likes and all one can do is to ask oneself after the event why it has happened in this way and no other.[3]

We think that retrospective specification of experiences that turn out in ways other than what we planned for is, or at least can be, a valuable educational experience in itself.

OBJECTIVES

If we can agree that "objective" is usually used to mean something like "aim," "end," "end-in-view," or "goal," then we can ask questions about 1) the beginning of the end, that is when the means stop and the end begins, and 2) the qualitative differences between possible objectives that are important to one's life and learning — differences that would suggest what sort of specification would be most appropriate to indicate their achievement. For example, a high school student could conceivably be concerned about "getting Antigone," "getting married," and "getting a quadratic equation right." These objectives do not, to all minds, suggest identical measures for their specification, achievement, or worth. Yet they are legitimate objectives, presumably held by members of the same educational program at the same time. Should they all be subject to specification? Should only the more easily specifiable one be allowed as part of the program? Do we have any reason to ask faculty members to commit themselves either to specify all objectives or not to specify any objectives?

This contrast serves as a sort of paradigm example of the humanist versus behaviorist quibble in its most innocent form. The challenge offered in the name of humanism is that the important things about life and learning are not subject to a process of specifying into objectives, and therefore, "specified objectives type" programs are destined to be unimportant or at least beside the point when it comes to personal meaning. This is met by the sallying behaviorist with the following: first of all, it is not clear that these "important things" (*Antigone*, marriage, feelings of integrity and comfort, and the like) cannot be broken down into objectives when properly understood; and in the second place, even though they are "important things," they do not belong in a formal instructional program designed for the acquisition of skills and knowledge.

Again, we think the controversy is unproductive, due mainly to a rather sloppy understanding of the concept *objective*. It seems to us that one can distinguish among three intimate but separate aspects of *objective:* intent, content, and sentiment. An illustration of this triadic separation might be found in the archer who 1) positions himself and takes aim, thereby behaviorally stating his intention with regard to the range and target; 2) delivers his arrow and marks its proximity to the intended objective, which would be the specified figure on the target field, thereby generating a measure of achievement relative to some sort of base (previous tries, other competitors, other bows and arrows, etc.); 3) experiences the empirical and existential facts of his performance, e.g., feels pride, disappointment, fatigue, invigoration, blood-lust for live targets, backache, fantasies of Sherwood Forest, etc., which may or may not relate directly to the intent or the content aspects of the *objective*, namely, to hit the mark with the arrow. If there is learning that occurs in this activity, it may be found in the aiming process, the scoring or measuring process (determination of content meaning), and in the after-play of responses to the activity as a whole. Or it may be found in a sequential combination of two or three of these aspects, in which case one end would serve as means to another end. It is important both to see that what we call means and ends can be considered *objectives* and to get out of the habit of treating *only* ends in this way.

It is possible to say that the "real objective"—that is, the one that is most important to the agent—is to be found in the transfer the agent develops by perfecting some sort of trajectory calculus, or it may be found in the success of making a preferred score regardless of the method used to make the shot (e.g., good results even with bad form, a practice that so often leads to the problems of sustained mediocrity suffered by natural athletes), or we may find it in the personal/social learning that takes place as one deliberates on the empirical and existential results of one's performance, whether good or bad, on or off target.

Clearly, all these emphases are important and relevant in most learning situations, albeit in different combinations at different times and in the different stages of educational development. It should be equally clear that all three aspects can be anticipated in virtually every learning activity; there will always be some intention, some content, and some affective response when learning occurs. This anticipation does not imply, however, that the various aspects of the objective under consideration can or should be pre-specified. It is difficult, for instance, to pre-specify how you want someone to feel after attempting to do something for the first time. (It should be mentioned that even though this is difficult, it is not always inappropriate. For instance, there may be good reason to engineer an experience of guaranteed frustration or failure in order to illustrate, to a person who unwittingly but regularly causes such experiences in others, what it *feels* like, in hopes of altering that person's understanding of his own behavior through altering his perceptions of the problem.[4])

We all set objectives whenever we think beyond the present with some intention. We accomplish some of them, discover new intentions along the way (perhaps in considering the content or sentiment resulting from the first intent), and accomplish some unintended things on the side (some important, some not). We cannot help setting objectives unless we give up the future and in so doing give up all choice and responsibility, plans, and hope. But at the same time, we cannot consciously anticipate all of the objectives we will serve, achieve, or even design. Still we can learn to recognize them as they occur or after they have occurred. Therein lie the most interesting problems, to us at least, of specifying objectives.

Education and its many objectives will never be reduced to a technology. Nevertheless, it is possible to think more precisely about the processes of teaching in ways that may be useful in planning educational activities. We have tried to add a dimension to the rather constricted picture of learning we get from the behavioral objectives point of view, by looking at the specification process from many angles. One conclusion that we draw is that the skills of specification, the discriminating disposition, and the ability to tell differences are central to many experiences that contribute to education.

CHAPTER TEN

Conclusion

OUR PURPOSE in this book has been to illuminate a common confusion and illustrate some of the consequences that follow from it. Insofar as this confusion between the roles of the schools in educating and socializing represents a problem for us, it is not the sort of problem that can be *solved*. These are distinctly different roles, supported by different and sometimes conflicting principles, that must be *accepted separately*. We believe it is a mistake to merge the two into a single unity because there is a tendency for one role (in this case, the role of educating) to become completely absorbed by the other.[1]

Even though we cannot solve this problem, we can nevertheless acknowledge that it exists and commit ourselves to keeping the distinction clear whenever it may be brought to bear upon particular cases. At present such a commitment implies a greater effort in preserving the schools' role in educating from being altogether absorbed into socialization.

As we noted in the first chapter, it is hardly novel to make some kind of distinction between educating and socializing, or schooling, or training. Many have done this before.[2] But none of them has made the distinction in quite the way that we have. This doesn't make us right and all the others wrong; it just means that we see things differently. We think, however, there is greater analytic utility in making the distinction as we have tried to do. It brings out the degree to which education continues to be eroded in our public schools, and the degree to which the democratic ideal of providing education for all has been undermined by confusing education and socialization.

It may be, of course, that many people are happy to use the schools merely to provide socialization for all—or, rather, would be happy if the schools could do even that. Schools in North America have been seen as instruments for shaping the children of diverse cultural backgrounds into competent social agents within the "new democracy" which is taken to be a single, general culture in its own right. This vision, which stresses the ideals of equality, has contributed to the tendency to collapse education into socialization. The conception of education that stresses individuality, the diversity among people, and the ability to tell differences, has even sometimes been seen as a covert threat to the ideals of equality that North American societies are struggling to realize. Although this struggle is often referred to as the struggle for "equal educational opportunity," a more accurate name would be "equal socialization opportunity."

Equality of socialization opportunity is an ideal that we might realistically move toward, using the Constitution, legislation, and the schools. We can, that is, hope to provide everyone with an equal opportunity to become socialized — to become competent social agents — by providing instruction in the basic tools of literacy, the means for earning a living, and the fundamentals of active citizenship. These are the aims of socialization. To confuse them with the aims of education, to call such a program "equal educational opportunity," is to confuse the different roles of the schools. It is this casual substitution of socialization for education in our language and in our thinking that prompted and perhaps justifies this book.

Notes

CHAPTER ONE: EDUCATION AND SOCIALIZATION

1. *On Further Examination* (Princeton: CEEB, 1977), p. 27.
2. *Ibid.*, p. 47.
3. *Ibid.*
4. For a discussion of this see A. J. Ayer, *The Origins of Pragmatism* (San Francisco: Freeman, Cooper, 1968), chapters 2, 3.
5. John Dewey, *Democracy and Education* (New York: Macmillan, 1916), p. 7.
6. *Ibid.*, p. 11.
7. *Ibid.*, p. 12.
8. *Ibid.*, p. 225.
9. *Ibid.*, p. 144.
10. *Ibid.*, p. 272.
11. *Ibid.*, p. 226.
12. John Dewey, *Philosophy of Education* (Patterson, N.J.: Littlefield, Adams and Co., 1958), p. 183.
13. *Democracy and Education*, p. 247.
14. *Ibid.*
15. *Ibid.*, p. 255.
16. *Ibid.*, p. 252.
17. *Ibid.*
18. *Ibid.*, p. 251.
19. *Ibid.*, pp. 253.

CHAPTER TWO: THE SOCIALIZATION OF SCHOOLS

1. For more on this theme see David Nyberg, "The Libertarian's McGuffey: A Review of Joel Spring's *A Primer of Libertarian Education*," *Urban Education*, 11 (1976), 465–70.
2. Benjamin N. Cardozo, *The Growth of the Law* (New Haven, Conn.: Yale University Press, 1924), p. 19.

3. Benjamin N. Cardozo, *The Nature of the Judicial Process* (New Haven, Conn.: Yale University Press, 1921), p. 43.
4. See Nathan Glazer, "Forword," in David L. Kirp and Mark G. Yudof, *Educational Policy and the Law* (Berkeley: McCutchan, 1974).
5. John Dewey, "Context and Thought," in his *On Experience, Nature, and Freedom*, ed. Richard H. Bernstein (Indianapolis, Ind.: Liberal Arts Press, 1960), p. 93.
6. Gilbert Ryle, *The Concept of Mind* (New York: Barnes and Noble, 1971), pp. 25–26.
7. Brown v. Board of Education, 347 U.S. 495 (1954).
8. George A. Kelly, *The Psychology of Personal Constructs* (New York: W. W. Norton, 1955), and Thomas S. Kuhn, *The Structure of Scientific Revolutions*, 2nd ed. (Chicago: University of Chicago Press, 1970).
9. Plato, *Republic*, Book VII.
10. John B. Watson, *Behaviorism* (New York: W. W. Norton, 1930). Of course, this kind of behavioral technology takes us quite far from our sense of education; it has to do with training and socialization.
11. For more detail see David Nyberg, "Pruning the Growth Metaphor," *Educational Forum*, 40 (1975), 23–31.
12. John Dewey, *Democracy and Education* (New York: Macmillan, 1916), pp. 49–50.
13. R. S. Peters, "Education as Initiation," in *Philosophical Analysis and Education*, ed. R. D. Archambault (London: Routledge and Kegan Paul, 1965), pp. 87–111.
14. Israel Scheffler, "Philosophical Models of Teaching," *Harvard Educational Review*, 34 (1965), 131–43. Scheffler's discussion of the impression and insight models of teaching was very helpful in developing this set of conceptions.
15. *Ibid.*, p. 140.
16. Alexander Pope, *Moral Essays, Epistle I*.
17. Brown v. Board of Education, 347 U.S. 493.
18. See, for example, Everett Reimer, *School Is Dead: Alternatives in Education* (Garden City, N.Y.: Doubleday, 1971), and Ivan Illich, *Deschooling Society* (New York: Harper & Row, 1971).
19. Robert Michels, *Political Parties: A Sociological Study of Oligarchical Tendencies of Modern Democracy* (New York: First International Library, 1915).
20. Wisconsin v.Yoder, 406 U.S. 205 (1972).
21. Joseph R. Gusfield, *Community: A Critical Response* (New York: Harper and Row, 1975) p. 30.
22. *Ibid.*, p. 34.
23. *Ibid.*, p. 35.
24. Serrano v. Priest, 4 Cal. 3d 584 (1971). However, see Joel S. Berke, "Recent Adventures of State School Finance: A Saga of Rocket Ships and Glider Planes," *School Review*, 82 (1974), 193–206, and James W. Guthrie, "School Finance Reform: Acceptable Remedies for Serrano," *School Review*, 82 (1975), 207–32, for discussions of some difficulties in this area.

25. Harry L. Summerfield, "The Limits of Federal Educational Policy," *Teachers College Record*, 76 (1974), 7–17.
26. For a full discussion of the involvement of the government in United States public education see J. Myron Atkin, "The Government in the Classroom," *Daedalus*, 109 (Summer 1980), 85–97.

CHAPTER THREE: THE NEED FOR EDUCATIONAL THEORY

1. Jean Piaget, *The Child and Reality* (New York: Penguin, 1976), p. 30.
2. J. W. Renner, in J. W. Renner, D. G. Stafford, A. E. Lawson, J. W McKinnon, F. E. Friot, and D. H. Kellogg, eds., *Research, Teaching and Learning with the Piaget Model* (Norman: University of Oklahoma Press, 1976), p. 4.
3. We realize that those sensitive to the associations of metaphors will find this use of *product* disturbing. In defence we would point out that we are hardly insensitive to the problems of "means-ends" prescriptions in education and are clearly not promoting such an image. Metaphors have uses and dangers. One danger is letting oversensitivity to a particular metaphoric image prevent one from seeing the limits of its application, and also prevent one from seeing the argument it is a part of.

CHAPTER FOUR: VARIETIES OF SOCIALIZATION

1. Alfred North Whitehead, *The Aims of Education* (London: Macmillan, 1929).
2. Matthew Arnold, *Culture and Anarchy* (1869; reprint ed., Cambridge: Cambridge University Press, 1957), p. 6.
3. Carl Bereiter, *Must We Educate?* (Englewood Cliffs, N.J.: Prentice-Hall, 1973).
4. *Ibid.*, p. 13.
5. *Ibid.*, p. 5.
6. Here we encounter our first difficulty with Bereiter's sometimes remiss use of words. *Dilemma* is normally held to mean a situation offering a choice of equally unsatisfactory alternatives, and not just indecision or speculation on an issue of indeterminate boundaries. If there is a dilemma here, Bereiter does not tell us what it is.
7. *Must We Educate?*, pp. 18, 76–77, 9, 8, 10.
8. *Ibid.*, p. 6.
9. *Ibid.*, p. 7.
10. Such a list might include the following: R. D. Archambault, ed., *Philosophical Analysis and Education* (London: Routledge and Kegan Paul, 1965); Harry S. Broudy, "Didactics, Heuristics, and Philetics," *Educational Theory*, 22, no. 3 (Summer 1972); R. F. Dearden, P. H. Hirst, and R. S. Peters, eds., *Education and the Development of Reason* (London:

Routledge and Kegan Paul, 1972); Thomas F. Green, *The Activities of Teaching* (New York: McGraw Hill, 1971); Maxine Greene, *Teacher as Stranger* (Belmont, California: Wadsworth, 1973); P. H. Hirst and R. S. Peters, eds., *The Logic of Education* (London: Routledge and Kegan Paul, 1970); David Nyberg, ed., *The Philosophy of Open Education* (London: Routledge and Kegan Paul, 1975); R. S. Peters, ed., *The Concept of Education* (London: Routledge and Kegan Paul, 1967); R. S. Peters, ed., *The Philosophy of Education* (London: Oxford University Press, 1973); Hugh G. Petrie, "The Believing in Seeing," in *Theories for Teaching*, ed. Lindley J. Stiles (New York: Dodd, Mead, 1974); Israel Scheffler, *The Language of Education* (Springfield, Ill.: Charles C. Thomas, 1960); B. Othanel Smith and Robert H. Ennis, eds., *Language and Concepts in Education* (Chicago: Rand McNally, 1961); I. A. Snook, ed., *Concepts of Indoctrination* (London: Routledge and Kegan Paul, 1972); Donald Vandenberg, ed., *Teaching and Learning* (Urbana: University of Illinois Press, 1969).

11. For example, Monroe C. Beardsley, *Thinking Straight* (Englewood Cliffs, N.J.: Prentice-Hall, 1966), chapter six; Max Black, *Critical Thinking* (Englewood Cliffs, N.J.: Prentice-Hall, 1952), chapter eleven; John Hospers, *An Introduction to Philosophical Analysis* (Englewood Cliffs, N.J.: Prentice-Hall, 1953), chapter one; and Israel Scheffler, *The Language of Education*.

12. *Must We Educate?*, p. 6.

13. In his arguments, Bereiter does not show the breadth of the notion of "skill." He does not advise us of the differences between capacities and tendencies as characteristics of different skills, nor of the distinction between "knowing how" skills that require practice, that are empirical and synthetic, and "knowing how" skills that are not contingent on practice, that are in a broad sense analytic. We refer the reader to Jane Roland Martin's "On the Reduction of 'Knowing That' to 'Knowing How'" in *Language and Concepts in Education*, ed. B. O. Smith and R. H. Ennis (Chicago: Rand McNally, 1961) for an excellent discussion of these distinctions. What he means by the term is simply doing something without moral implication, a dubious proposition of the first order.

14. *Must We Educate?*, p. 18.

15. Carl R. Rogers, *Freedom to Learn* (Columbus, Ohio: Charles E. Merrill, 1969), p. 269.

16. *Must We Educate?*, p. 8.

17. *Freedom to Learn*, p. 153.

18. Israel Scheffler, "Philosophical Models of Teaching," in his *Reason and Thinking* (London: Routledge and Kegan Paul, 1973), p. 68. This chapter originally appeared under the same title in *Harvard Educational Review*, 34 (1965), 131–43.

19. *Ibid.*, pp. 69–70.

20. *Ibid.*, p. 71.

21. *Ibid.*

22. *Ibid.*, p. 72.

23. *Ibid.*, p. 75.
24. *Ibid.*, p. 76.
25. *Ibid.*, p. 77.
26. *Ibid.*, p. 76.
27. See T. F. Daveny's essay, "Education—A Moral Concept" in *New Essays in the Philosophy of Education*, ed. G. Langford and D. J. O'Connor (London: Routledge and Kegan Paul, 1973).
28. *Must We Educate?*, p. 34.
29. Robert R. Sherman, *Democracy, Stoicism and Education* (Gainesville: University of Florida Press, 1973), pp. 46–47.
30. *Must We Educate?*, p. 22.

CHAPTER FIVE: TOWARD AN EDUCATIONAL THEORY

1. David P. Ausubel, "Viewpoints from Related Disciplines: Human Growth and Development," *Teachers College Record*, 60 (1959), 245–54.
2. *Ibid.*, p. 246.
3. Alfred North Whitehead, "The Rhythm of Education" in his *The Aims of Education* (London: Macmillan, 1929; reprint ed., New York: The Free Press, 1967).
4. Iona and Peter Opie, *Children's Games in Street and Playground* (Oxford: Clarendon Press, 1969), p. 4. For further discussion of games in education, and an excellent biography, see Elliott M. Avedon and Brian Sutton-Smith, *The Study of Games* (New York: John Wiley and Sons, 1971), pp. 315–46. See also Brian Sutton-Smith, *The Folkgames of Children* (Austin: University of Texas Press, 1972), and Jean Piaget, *The Moral Judgement of the Child*, trans. Marjorie Gabain (New York: The Free Press, 1965).
5. See, for example, K. Bühler, *The Mental Development of the Child*, trans. Oscar Oeser (London: Routledge and Kegan Paul, 1930), and Bruno Bettleheim, *The Uses of Enchantment* (New York: Knopf, 1976).
6. For development of this argument see Frank Kermode, *The Sense of an Ending* (London: Oxford University Press, 1966), and Kieran Egan, "What Is a Plot?" *New Literary History*, 10 (Spring 1978).
7. For some analyses of mythic thinking useful in this context see Bronislaw Malinowski, *Myth in Primitive Psychology*, rpt. in *Magic, Science, and Religion* (New York: Doubleday, 1954); Mircea Eliade, *Myth and Reality* (New York: Harper and Row, 1963); and Claude Lévi-Strauss, *The Savage Mind* (Chicago: University of Chicago Press, 1966), *Structural Anthropology* (New York: Basic Books, 1963), and *The Raw and the Cooked* (New York: Harper and Row, 1969).
8. See Roman Jakobson and M. Halle, *Fundamentals of Language* (The Hague: Mouton, 1956).
9. J. Piaget, "Children's Philosophies" in *Handbook of Child Psychology*, ed. C. Murchison (Worcester, Mass.: Clark University Press, 1931), p. 382.

10. K. Bühler, *The Mental Development of the Child*. The reference appears often throughout the book.

11. *Ibid*.

12. This might seem a regression rather than a development. The "philosophic" generalizations might seem very crude and simple-minded compared with the complexity of the "romantic" organization of some phenomenon. But it is the generation of very abstract concepts that will eventually permit much more powerful and refined organization. Romantic stage organizing lacks the power of "philosophic" general schemes, and lacks the potential for bringing diverse phenomena into complex processes.

13. For an elaborated version of the theory sketched in this chapter, see Kieran Egan, *Educational Development* (New York: Oxford University Press, 1979).

CHAPTER SIX: TEACHING AND BELIEVING

1. For a pro-and-con introduction, see K. Ryan and D. Purpel, eds., *Moral Education* (Berkeley: McCutchan, 1976), especially part II.

2. Michael Scriven, *Primary Philosophy* (New York: McGraw-Hill, 1966), p. 2.

3. Friedrich Nietzsche, *Beyond Good and Evil*, I. 6. The Kaufmann translation (New York: Random House, 1966) has "memoir" where the Zimmern translation (New York: Modern Library, 1954) has "autobiography."

4. G. J. Warnock, *English Philosophy Since 1900*, 2nd ed. (Oxford: Oxford University Press, 1969), p. 42.

5. J. P. Corbett, "Teaching Philosophy Now," in *Philosophical Analysis and Education*, ed. R.D. Archambault (London: Routledge and Kegan Paul, 1965), p. 150.

6. George A. Kelly, *The Psychology of Personal Constructs*, vol. 1 (New York: Norton, 1955), pp. 8–9.

7. Kenneth Boulding, *The Image* (Ann Arbor: University of Michigan Press, 1956).

8. W. V. Quine and J. S. Ullian, *The Web of Belief*, 2nd ed. (New York: Random House, 1970), p. 10.

9. John Dewey, *On Experience, Nature, and Freedom*, ed. R. J. Bernstein (Indianapolis: Liberal Arts Press, 1960), chapter IV, "Context and Thought."

10. "The next step in this process" is not strictly implied by the Belief Profile. It should properly be the function of the interaction, or transaction, between the teacher, the Profile, and the student. An example of a possible, and feasible, "next step" would be to assign three to five students who show similar belief clusters to meet together in order to discuss the first assigned readings, and to reinforce each other's beliefs. Then pit one of

these groups against another, which represents a conflicting cluster of held beliefs on generally the same issue, and ask them to debate the issue. In this way, the teacher could assess the degree to which the students understood the assigned reading and, by implication, their own beliefs, and he or she could point out, using the debate as an example, how difficult and emotion-laden discussion of philosophical issues can become, especially when dealt with on the level of beliefs.

CHAPTER SEVEN: BELIEFS AND THE EDUCATIONAL CURRICULUM

1. B. A. van Groningen, *In the Grip of the Past* (Leiden, The Netherlands: E. J. Brill, 1953), p. 3.
2. William K. Frankena, *Philosophy of Education* (New York: Macmillan, 1965).
3. *Ibid.*, pp. 19–25.
4. *Ibid.*, pp. 26–36.
5. *Ibid.*, pp. 37–43.
6. *Ibid.*, pp. 44–51.
7. Decker F. Walker, "Straining to Lift Ourselves," *Curriculum Theory Network*, 5, no. 1 (1975), 5.

CHAPTER EIGHT: TEACHING, INSTRUCTING, AND THEIR DIFFERENT OBJECTIVES

1. See, for example, Michael Duncan and Bruce Biddle, *The Study of Teaching* (New York: Holt, Rinehart and Winston, 1974).
2. N. L. Gage, *The Scientific Basis of the Art of Teaching* (New York: Teachers College Press, 1978), p. 18.
3. *Ibid.*, p. 91.
4. Jerome S. Bruner, *Towards a Theory of Instruction* (Cambridge, Mass.: The Belknap Press of Harvard University Press, 1966). Some elaboration of his model has appeared but in general this scheme is widely accepted.
5. *Ibid.*, p. 40.
6. This particular question is raised as an example because this is precisely and explicitly what is happening in a number of Piagetian programs. See Deanna Kuhn, "The Application of Piaget's Theory of Cognitive Development to Education," *Harvard Educational Review*, 49 (1979), 340–60.
7. As Richard C. Atkinson puts it, "The learning models that now exist are totally inadequate to explain the subtle ways by which the human organism stores, processes, and retrieves information" ("Ingredients for a Theory of Instruction," *American Psychologist*, 27 [1972], 929).

8. Lee J. Cronbach, "The Two Disciplines of Scientific Psychology," *American Psychologist*, 12 (1957), 11; "Beyond the Two Disciplines of Scientific Psychology," *American Psychologist*, 30 (1975), 2.
9. "The Two Disciplines of Scientific Psychology," p. 681.
10. "Beyond the Two Disciplines of Scientific Psychology," p. 119.
11. *Ibid.*, p. 119.
12. *Ibid.*, p. 125.
13. *Ibid.*, p. 126.
14. Richard Snow, "Individual Differences and Instructional Theory," *Educational Researcher*, 6 (1977), 12.
15. *Ibid.*
16. Roger Gehlbach, "Individual Differences: Implications for Instructional Theory, Research, and Innovation," *Educational Researcher*, 8 (April, 1979), 8–14.
17. *Ibid.*, p. 12.
18. G. Pask and B. C. E. Scott, "Learning Strategies and Individual Competence," *International Journal of Man-Machine Studies*, 4 (1972), 217–53.
19. Atkinson, "Ingredients for a Theory of Instruction," p. 923.
20. See W. J. Popham, Elliot W. Eisner, Howard J. Sullivan, and Louise Tyler, *Instructional Objectives* (Chicago: Rand McNally, 1969).
21. For a discussion of some of these problems see Hugh Sockett, "Curriculum Aims and Objectives: Taking a Means to an End," *Proceedings of the Philosophy of Education Society of Great Britain* (Oxford: Basil Blackwell, 1972), pp. 30–61.
22. Another strange feature of the "behavioral objectives movement," and its associated "accountability movement," and the growth of "evaluation" to the point where it seems a larger enterprise than education, is the sources of their support. This too is outside our argument, but it seems worth noting that much of the support for these movements comes from people who nevertheless find them simplistic and distasteful. Many people see these movements as weapons against the mindless "do your own thing" proposals which proliferated in education particularly in the 1960s. An aging band of more or less ex-radical professors still promote the old nonsense and their old opponents see what they would be happy to call the new nonsense as a useful temporary antidote to their lingering influence. Thus they applaud school districts that demand that all teachers state the objectives of their courses in behavioral terms, and that impose rigorous evaluation of their success. These procedures are not of a kind that such professors would recommend in their ideal educational system, but they see them as regrettable allies in a contemporary struggle. We think they may get more than they bargain for.
23. W. James Popham, *Criterion-Referenced Instruction* (Belmont, Calif.: Fearon, 1973), p. 13.
24. Robert Mager, *Behavioral Objectives* (Belmont, Calif.: Fearon, 1962), p. 13.
25. W. James Popham and Eva L. Baker, *Systematic Instruction* (Englewood Cliffs, N.J.: Prentice-Hall, 1979), p. 20.

26. See, for example, Phillippe C. Duchastel and Paul F. Merrill, "The Effects of Behavioral Objectives on Learning: A Review of Empirical Studies," *Review of Educational Research*, 43 (1973), 53–69, and O. K. Duell, "Effect of Type of Objective, Level of Test Questions, and the Judged Importance of Tested Materials upon Post-Test Performance," *Journal of Educational Psychology*, 66 (1974), 225–32.

CHAPTER NINE: EDUCATIONAL OBJECTIVES

1. B. F. Skinner, *Beyond Freedom and Dignity* (New York: Knopf, 1971); see chapters 7–8.
2. Alan Watts, *The Book* (New York: Pantheon, 1966), p. 39.
3. Sigmund Freud, *The Complete Introductory Lectures on Psychoanalysis* (New York: Norton, 1966), p. 379.
4. See David Nyberg, *Tough and Tender Learning* (Palo Alto, Calif.: National Press Books, 1971), especially chapter 7, "A Valuable Waste of Time."

CHAPTER TEN: CONCLUSION

1. For a discussion of this see David Nyberg, "Explaining Education," *Curriculum Inquiry*, 11 (Summer 1981), 175–87.
2. For a list of a number of ways one might distinguish between education and socialization, see Pat White, "Socialization and Education" in *Education and the Development of Reason*, ed., R. F. Dearden, P. H. Hirst, and R. S. Peters (London: Routledge and Kegan Paul, 1972), pp. 113–31.

Index